WRITERS AND THEIR WORK

ISOBEL ARMSTRONG
General Editor

BRYAN LOUGHREY
Advisory Editor

Henry Fielding

HENRY FIELDING

from a sketch by HOGARTH *used as a frontispiece to the Works, 1762*

Henry
Fielding

Jenny Uglow

Northcote House

in association with
The British Council

For John Barnard

© Copyright 1995 by Jenny Uglow

First published in 1995 by Northcote House Publishers Ltd, Plymbridge House,
Estover Road, Plymouth PL6 7PZ, United Kingdom.
Tel: (01752) 735251. Fax: (01752) 695699.

British Library Cataloguing-in-Publication Data
A catalogue record for this book is available from the British Library

ISBN 0 7463 0748 9

Typeset by PDQ Typesetting, Newcastle-Under-Lyme
Printed and bound in the United Kingdom by BPC Wheatons Ltd, Exeter

Contents

Acknowledgements

Writing on Fielding has been hugely enjoyable, and I am grateful for the insights of critics, biographers, and scholars, past and present. More specifically I am indebted to Isobel Armstrong, Claude Rawson, and Kate Teltscher for their encouragement and their valuable comments, to Steve Uglow for his help with eighteenth-century criminal process, and to Hilary Walford for her meticulous copy-editing. In particular, I would like to thank Hermione Lee and John Barnard for many stimulating conversations, and for a quality that Fielding greatly valued, the gift of friendship.

Biographical Outline

1747–8	Edits the *Jacobite's Journal*.
1748	Becomes Justice of the Peace for Westminster.
1749	*Tom Jones*. Justice of the Peace for Middlesex.
1751	*An Enquiry into the Causes of the late Increase of Robbers; Amelia*.
1752	Edits the *Covent-Garden Journal*.
1753	*A Proposal for Making an Effectual Provision for the Poor*.
1754	Revised version of *Jonathan Wild*. Resigns from position as Justice because of ill health: dies near Lisbon in Portugal, 8 October.
1755	*The Journal of a Voyage to Lisbon*, published posthumously.

Abbreviations and References

Wherever possible I have quoted from the authoritative Wesleyan Edition of Fielding's works which is gradually being produced by the Clarendon Press (see Bibliography), and, for consistency, I have followed their style throughout. Works not covered by the Wesleyan can be found in various editions, the most complete being W. E. Henley (1903).

However, for ease of reference, page numbers for the novels apply to paperback editions of Fielding's fiction currently in print, or to recent critical editions of the plays, where they exist. Readers may find that these texts vary slightly from the source quoted, particularly with regard to modernized spelling, punctuation, and capitalization.

The list below notes editions for which page numbers (or, in the case of the plays, act and scene numbers) are given.

A.   *Amelia* (Harmondsworth: Penguin, 1987)

AF   *The Author's Farce* (London: Edward Arnold, 1967)

C.   *Champion* (London: Heinemann, 1903)

CGJ   *Covent-Garden Journal* (Oxford: Clarendon Press, 1988)

CGT   *The Covent-Garden Tragedy* (London: Heinemann, 1903)

DQE   *Don Quixote in England* (London: Heinemann, 1903)

E.   *An Enquiry into the Causes of the late Increase of Robbers* (Oxford: Clarendon Press, 1988)

EH   *Eurydice Hiss'd* included with *The Historical Register* (London: Edward Arnold, 1968)

FH   *The Female Husband and Other Writings* (Liverpool: Liverpool University Press, 1960)

GSO   *The Grub-Street Opera* (London: Edward Arnold, 1969)

HR   *The Historical Register for the Year 1736* (London: Edward Arnold, 1968)

IT   *The Intriguing Chambermaid* (London: Heinemann, 1903)

J.   *A Journey from This World to the Next* (London: Dent

(Everyman), 1973).

JA/S	*Joseph Andrews and Shamela* (Oxford: Oxford University Press (World's Classics), 1980)
JL	*The Journal of a Voyage to Lisbon*, in *Jonathan Wild* (London: Dent (Everyman), 1973)
JW	*Jonathan Wild* (Harmondsworth: Penguin, 1982)
M.	*Miscellanies I* (Oxford: Clarendon Press, 1972)
MD	*The Mock Doctor* (London: Heinemann, 1903)
P.	*Pasquin* (London: Heinemann, 1903)
TJ	*Tom Jones* (Harmondsworth: Penguin, 1966)
TT	*The Tragedy of Tragedies and Tom Thumb* (London: Oliver and Boyd, 1973)

Prologue

'Containing five Pages of Paper.'

'Of Love.'

'A most dreadful Chapter indeed; and which few Readers ought to
venture upon in an Evening, especially when alone.'

'An Apology for all Heroes who have good Stomachs, with a
Description of a Battle of the amorous Kind.'

'A Crust for the Critics.'

The sly, dashing chapter headings of *Tom Jones* are a clue to the
delight and surprise of reading Henry Fielding. His throw-away
lines at once embrace and distance the reader, conveying his
enjoyment in playing with a form which he himself has partly
invented, his fun in the mock-heroic battles, his defiance of 'the
critics', his sudden swoops to seriousness, his high-spirited love
of the absurd. In Fielding's work the manipulative puppet-master
rarely disappears behind the screens, but even though we are
constantly aware of his authorial presence we are not bullied by a
single dominating view, since he himself puts on different masks,
at one point addressing our intellect, at another appealing to our
sense of moral outrage, at another touching our emotions.

Fielding's characteristic style blends realistic and symbolic
writing – the 'Emblematical' mode, as a character in his play
Pasquin describes it. The reader is asked, simultaneously, to
suspend disbelief, surrendering to the plot and caring about the
characters, and yet to remain sceptical, analysing the allegory
with a clear mind. We thus partake in the action and also share in
the conscious ordering (and judging) of a potentially chaotic
world. Fielding's ironic control also implies the force of that
which must be controlled: the possibility of wild, surreal flights; of
energy under restraint; of dangerous passions and anarchic

1

conflicts. In *Joseph Andrews* for example – a novel which seems fluidly 'Quixotic' in more ways than one, yet is tightly and cunningly structured – Fielding repeatedly lets the action build to the brink of chaos, then twists events, not to a conclusion, but to 'interrupt' and divert the flowing narrative into another channel. He claims that his novels are true 'Histories' in comparison to earlier romances – they represent the real. But at the same time, the skilful, very visible manipulation of his narrative implies that all their resolutions of untractable problems are, in themselves, 'fictions'.

Fielding, as author, both performs and directs. Anthony Burgess once described his career as 'a play in four Acts': the first act, played out in the 1730s, won him fame as a playwright and also as an experimental theatre manager. At every turn in his career – as dramatist, journalist, novelist, and magistrate – we feel that rapid, directing intelligence. He is a great innovator, watching and pouncing on new ideas, new forms, making practical plans (from the building of new theatres to the reduction of London's crime) as well as pushing the boundaries of artistic forms.

Fielding, however, never plucks his ideas out of the void. His originality consists in adapting recent developments and past models to create new forms: it is fascinating to watch his circling dance with his great (and jealous) rival Samuel Richardson, both deriding yet learning from the other. As a satirist, although his tone is more genial, he saw himself as the successor of Pope and Swift, signing some of his early works 'Scriblerus Secundus' or 'Lemuel Gulliver'. As a serious dramatist he reworked the Restoration comedies of manners and sentiment, while his 'irregular dramas' are an inventive mix of current forms: topical satire, farce, burlesque, ballad opera, and street puppet show. In both plays and novels he develops the use of 'humours', derived from medieval medicine and modified in Elizabethan drama, into a fully-fleshed allegorical mode, reflecting complicated social relationships through a mosaic of exaggerated characteristics.

This aspect of his work – achieving criticism through ridicule, without losing touch with humanity – was partly learnt from his heroes, Molière, Cervantes, and Swift. But he also looked back to far older models and these form part of his moral, as well as artistic universe: the sense of being rooted in traditions gives his writing solidity and resonance. Episodes from the Bible and the

Classics, in particular the *Iliad* and the *Odyssey*, glint behind his plots. His comic drama recalls Plautus and, at its most bizarre and politically pointed, Aristophanes. The strangeness and force of *Jonathan Wild*, or of *A Journey from This World to the Next*, derive partly from the Greek writer Lucian.

It is this allusive aspect of his work, so rich and familiar to his first readers, that we are most likely to miss. His irony, and his flashing, life-loving humour make him accessible, and his experimental shifts between realism and expressionism are in tune with modern practice (sometimes he even seems like a deft, knowing postmodernist). But he is anchored in his age, and the deep, allusive patterns of his writing are harder to grasp, used as we are to the self-contained worlds and penetrative psychology of Victorian and modern novels. To adapt another chapter title from *Tom Jones* – 'In which the history runs backwards' – it is like plunging from planes and trains, suburbs and streets, through the tangled woods and secret gardens of the nineteenth century and leaping over a wall into a pre-enclosure landscape, open and unfenced, yet subject to complex ancient laws, inscribed in the consciousness of the inhabitants.

The forms Fielding worked in are moulded to his vision, whether it be critical (like the 'rehearsal' play with its layering of self-display and deception) or benign (the fictional journey, with its fits and starts, reversals and accidents and happy ending). He wrote fast, but never uses language casually, since he sees abuse of words as symptomatic of the abuses of his time: in his journal the *Champion*, he quotes John Locke:

> Whoever shall consider the Errors and Obscurity, the Mistakes and Confusion, that are spread in the World by an ill use of Words, will find some Reason to doubt, whether Language as it has been employed, has contributed more to the Improvement or Hindrance of Knowledge amongst Mankind. (C. 159)

Hence his disgust with Richardson's use of 'Virtue' in *Pamela*, which he parodies as the degenerated form 'Vartue' in *Shamela*.

In Fielding's work a broad, zestful European heritage blends with stubbornly patriotic and local loyalties: the most popular song he wrote, sung throughout the eighteenth century, was 'The Roast Beef of Old England'. The authors he admired provided him (as they did Swift) less with a reverence for authority than with authority to be irreverent, with the sense that it is an author's duty to expose cant and affectation, to uphold principles of right against those who would subvert them. Fielding came from the rural gentry, laid claim to aristocratic forebears, and worked his influential connections hard, yet his is a very democratic art.

This is true in a profound, rather than a loosely political sense: he was no egalitarian leveller. In essence, in tune with many of his peers – whether they were Tories, like Swift and Pope, or 'patriotic' Whigs – Fielding was fighting for values which he felt were being threatened on several fronts: by new styles of government, sustained by influence rather than merit; by new financial networks dependent on credit and speculation and bolstered by the taste for 'luxury'; by new ways of thinking, ideas which undercut old religious and social models.

Fielding thus treads a difficult path between conservative and progressive tendencies. As a magistrate he worked for reform, but administered the current laws and imposed their harsh penalties. And, although Joseph Andrews and Tom Jones are a servant and a 'foundling' who eventually benefit from fairy-tale good fortune, he never questions (or thinks of questioning) the established class order. His attitude towards the poor is complicated; he relishes the noisy, gutsy zest of popular culture yet admires gentility and polish; he asserts equality of goodness yet sees the mob as a threatening monster of disorder. Moreover, his is a very male viewpoint: women scholars are the butt of many jokes and his poem 'To a friend on the Choice of a Wife' proposes an ideal woman who is tender, sensual, and good-natured – but knows her place:

> Superior Judgment may she own thy Lot;
> Humbly advise, but contradict thee not.'

(M. 50)

His fictional ideal, however, the Sophia in *Tom Jones* (based on his own wife), is critical of Tom and contradicts him all the time. She is spirited and resourceful as well as beautiful and pure.

When Fielding paints the near-ruin of a family in his last, sombre novel, *Amelia*, he shows the 'submissive' heroine as the true source of strength. Corruption almost always comes from above and the worst offence is the abnegation of responsibility and the abuse of power. He grew up defying authority, and all his works denounce the selfish clinging to power, whether it be parental, marital, sexual, financial, legal, or political. The 'Great'

Jonathan Wild (and, by analogy, Robert Walpole) is not a villain because he is a thief but because his self-important lust for fame leads others to death and ruin. He believed in the guiding hand of providence, in salvation by good works, and in the essential goodness of human nature. But he saw how hard it was to reconcile such ideas with the realities of history and the problems of the contemporary world, and his satire often strikes simultaneously at the predatory evils of the old code of 'heroic' martial honour and aristocratic pride and at the meshes of the new (but equally self-interested) legal, mercantile, and financial web.

The splits and swerves in Fielding's work mime the obsessions and divisions of his time. Part of his genius is his ability to find new modes to express new confidence. He works and weaves and jokes across the map of recent history. In the background, since the 'Glorious Revolution' of 1688 had expelled the Stuart James II and brought William and Mary to the throne, lay the threat of Jacobite revolt, the fear of 'Popery', and the lasting hostility to the French. The foreground was cluttered with intense, factional party politics. After the death of Queen Anne in 1714, the arrival of the Hanoverian George I from Germany, and the collapse of the Jacobite rebellion the following year, Tory power effectively collapsed and a long period of Whig supremacy began. But among the Whigs were more factions, hardening into the fierce opposition to Robert Walpole's government in the 1730s. And, although executive power had passed significantly from the monarchy to the great landed magnates, the constitutional revolution of the 1680s had been followed by a financial one, with the establishment of the Bank of England, the National Debt; and the Stock Market. Over the next fifty years the demands of the wars on the Continent – the Nine Years War (1689–97), the War of Spanish Succession (1702–13), and the War of Austrian Succession (1739–48), – meant that the support of the merchant community was vital. The uneasy accord between aristocratic, City, and professional influences was welded within a new urban élite: 'polite society' or 'the Town' (often the target of Fielding's jibes). But the stormy debates of the era, as well as its political and social tensions, are inscribed in Fielding's novels and plays. Disputes rose like steam from the crowded coffee-houses and London clubs, from the satirical pamphlets and poems, the journals and tracts: in the decades after the ending of the

Licensing Act of 1695 'public opinion' had become a new, powerful force.

In terms of political philosophy, by and large Fielding upheld the ideals of civic humanism, as expressed by Anthony Ashley Cooper, 3rd Earl of Shaftesbury, in his *Characteristics of Men, Manners, Opinions and Times* (1711). Building on earlier theorists, Shaftesbury looked to classical Roman republicanism as a model (as did Pope, Addison, Steele, Swift, and other leading writers of the self-dubbed 'Augustan age', invoking the era of Caesar Augustus and Virgil, Horace and Ovid). Shaftesbury's ideal state was paternalistic and hierarchical, ruled by disinterested public men. He saw society as a moral entity, in which the ethics of government were linked to the virtues of the population: thrift, hard work, liberty, and heroism could build a healthy body politic, while luxury and corruption would infect and destroy it. Beneath this vision lay a benign view of human nature, since men's 'affections', in Shaftesbury's view, were not merely selfish appetites but channels of fellowship and social cohesion: 'a public spirit can only come from a social feeling or sense of partnership with human kind.'[1] Personal virtue and public spirit could both be fostered by education and philosophy.

In sharp contrast to this optimistic belief in human fellowship, another strand of thought drew on the writings of Thomas Hobbes, who saw mankind as essentially selfish, and culture and religion as vital means of civilizing the crude, 'fallen' instincts of self-preservation. As Hobbes famously said, if left in a 'natural', uncultured state, man's life would be 'solitary, poore, nastie, brutish and short'.[2] This conviction underlay Bernard de Mandeville's controversial satire, *The Fable of the Bees*, published in successive editions in 1714, 1723, and 1729. With startling bluntness, Mandeville declared that no trading state, as Britain now was, could honestly claim that its aim was altruism rather than profit. The moral language of political debate was hypocritical and should be dropped: 'luxury' was not necessarily a vice, more a useful means of stimulating demand and creating work, while religion and 'politeness' were mere tactics to sweeten self-interest and oil the wheels of the economy. As an invented correspondent in Fielding's the *Champion* put it, from this perspective masks are invaluable and deceit inevitable, since, 'Virtue is a sort of Cash unknown to the Butcher, the Baker, the

Draper, the Tailor. If a Man carries nothing but Virtue to Market, he will, I am afraid carry nothing else from it' (C.171).

These arguments buzzed through fashionable thinking circles in the 1720s and 1730s, and one can trace them throughout Fielding's work; he is still arguing with Mandeville in *Amelia*, as late as 1751. Many of his characters do use 'manners', or religious cant, to hide 'brutish' greed, but this must not, he insists, cancel our faith in human nature. The competing ideas are also related to the way Fielding depicts *choice*. Are we in control of our lives, or are they ruled by 'Providence', or constrained by laws, by economics, by temperament? Writing on art, Shaftesbury had said that 'history painting' (considered the highest form), should make its classical or biblical subjects relevant to present dilemmas. His chosen example was the judgement of Hercules between Virtue and Pleasure (usually shown as two beautiful women). Fielding's 'histories', as he called them, echo this shape: epic forms hover behind modern problems, as Joseph Andrews, Tom Jones, and Billy Booth find themselves caught between women representing different approaches to life.

But the key issue, to which Fielding returns again and again as an essential first step to correct judgement and choice of action, is the need to distinguish between public face and private motive. Even before he began his career as a dramatist in the 1730s, Fielding was fascinated by the disguises, scripts, and costumes people adopted to survive and to control others. Hobbes's *Leviathan* (1651) had dwelt on the problem of judging by outward appearance, 'which disguiseth the face as a mask or Visard', and had pointed to the link between person and *persona*, the Latin word originally used for an actor's mask: 'So that a *person*, is the same thing that an *actor* is, both on the stage and in common conversation, and to *personate* is to act, or *represent* himself or another.'[3] This suggestive remark immediately tosses up issues of literary, as well as social, 'representation' of identity. Fielding's fiction traces the plight and triumph of those who play no part but themselves, acting on, and acting out, their principles – Joseph Andrews and Abraham Adams, the Heartfrees, Tom Jones and Amelia Booth. In his fiercest moments, as in his 'Essay on the Knowledge of the Characters of Men', written in his mid-thirties, he depicts modern life as one great dance of deception:

> Thus while the crafty and designing Part of Mankind, consulting only their own separate Advantage, endeavour to maintain one constant Imposition on others, the whole World becomes a vast Masquerade, where the greatest Part appear disguised under false Vizors and Habits; a very few only shewing their own Faces, who become, by so doing, the Astonishment and Ridicule of all the rest. (*M.*55)

Fielding's comedy exposes vanity, sham, political duplicity, and religious narrowness, showing how egotism and self-deception inevitably efface sympathy: it confronts evil on behalf of good. But although his ridicule can be damning, in the end he is humane rather than savage, since he enjoys his creations – even in the disruptive force of the masquerade – and is all too aware of his own, as well as their, fallibility. That fallibility is a great part of his charm, for the recklessness that got this large, loose-limbed, fast-talking man into trouble with women, into fights, into debt (and sometimes into gaol) is a potent element in his art. He mocks himself – and his readers – as much as his targets. His characters may be emblems, wearing their names like placards, but they are also well-observed men and women with desires and dreams, bodies and appetites. In an early essay 'On Eating', written in 1736, he wrote:

> But tho' I cannot think that the *ultimate End* of Man is to *eat*, and that his whole Ambition shou'd be in extending the *Circumference* of his *Body*...yet I freely allow that there is a good deal of *Pleasure* in *Eating*, which reasonably may be indulg'd; for, as in the Performance of any Office of Nature, there must be a sensible and necessary Pleasure attend it, how is it possible to satisfy Hunger without enjoying that Pleasure?[4]

Hunger and Pleasure are often joined in Fielding's fiction: a bald admission of human needs and a buoyant, exuberant excess. Although he was more worldly-wise, I like to think there is something of Fielding himself in the picture of the combative, idealistic Abraham Adams – flailing his arms, clutching his Aeschylus, leaping over the downs crying 'Aye, aye, catch me if you can' – while the stage-coach, the lumbering British establishment, full of prissy, purse-lipped hypocrites, tries vainly to catch up.

1

Youth, Plays, and Politics

1

Fielding's life is peculiarly relevant to criticism of his work since one of the chief accusations levelled at him by rivals like Richardson was that his writing was autobiographical – he was a mere reporter, with no invention or genius. What was more, it was alleged that his subjects were invariably 'low' and vulgar, in keeping with the way he lived. Biographical fact thus becomes a facet of literary theory, of arguments about the nature and purpose of imaginative representation.

Henry Fielding was born in 1707 at Sharpham Park, Somerset, within sight of Glastonbury Tor – part of the setting for *Tom Jones* – but when he was 3 his family moved to East Stour, in Dorset. It was the estate here, running through meadows to the river, that he always thought of as home. Biographers like to suggest that Fielding's paradoxical blend of probity and wildness, striving and hedonism, was somehow bred into his genes. His mother, Sarah, was the daughter of a judge, and her family, the Goulds, were old-established Somerset gentry, while the Fieldings, who traced their line (falsely) back to the Hapsburgs, were notoriously intemperate and unpredictable.

Henry's father, Edmund Fielding, was an attractive, reckless soldier who eventually reached the rank of Lieutenant-Colonel, but was renowned for his gambling, womanizing, and debts. Henry was the first of eight children, but Edmund spent more time in London coffee-houses than with his growing family, and soon after Sarah died in 1718 he married the keeper of a London eating-house, an Italian, Roman Catholic widow. The Goulds were aghast, fearful of her Popish influence (the Jacobite invasion of 1715 still haunted English minds). After fierce court battles,

Henry's grandmother Lady Gould won custody of the children. Henry, aged 12, was sent to Eton – which he refers to in his novels as much for its fierce beatings as for its teaching of the Classics.

Fielding would always be drawn to the 'foundlings' of this world, and sensitive to the duties and aberrances of fathers. He was also determined, sometimes arrogantly so, to make his own way. He remained nostalgically fond of East Stour, but was so hopeless with money that he threw this inheritance away. As a youth he was loving and hot-tempered: in 1725, a year after leaving Eton, he fell precipitously in love with a distant relative, Sarah Andrew, whom he pursued to Lyme Regis. Her uncle, Andrew Tucker, had him beaten; Fielding tried to abduct her, failed, threatened Tucker, and was bound over to keep the peace: furious, he pinned a notice to the church door, to 'give notice to all the world' that Tucker and his son were 'clowns and cowards'. Two years later, aged 20, he was in London, giving notice to all the world of his arrival.

George I had died the previous year, and George II was now on the throne, ruled himself, so people said, by his wife, Caroline, staunch ally of Robert Walpole, First Lord of the Treasury (equivalent to the modern Prime Minister). Walpole had grasped power in 1720 by extricating the government from the South Sea Bubble crisis and had consolidated his position through patronage on an unprecedented scale, making sure that his placemen permeated the hierarchy from the Lord Chancellor to the lowest local official. Walpole was one of the butts of *Gullivers Travels* (1726), but when Fielding came to town two years later, although he admired Swift, his first published verses were an undistinguished Coronation ode and poem on the King's birthday. This suggests that initially he was hoping to make his fortune at court. He had useful connections there, especially his forceful, witty cousin, Lady Mary Wortley Montagu, but he was never destined to be a court favourite. Even at this early stage he looked like a maverick, a potential fount of danger, and within a few years he would be ostentatiously identified with the opposition to Walpole.

The year of Fielding's arrival, 1728, was in some ways a cultural turning-point. It was the year of Pope's *Dunciad*, but also of John Gay's *The Beggar's Opera*, and William Hogarth's intriguing series of paintings of that play and its audience. The theatrical and painted versions of *The Beggar's Opera* have been seen as representing 'the transition between the literary world of Dryden, Swift, and Pope and that of Fielding, Richardson, Sterne and Johnson'. In Ronald Paulson's words, 'Together Gay and Hogarth showed the way that satire, irony, allusion and analogy could be modified into a more generous and wide-ranging, in some ways more sentimental but in others more questioning and skeptical mode.'[1]

In his first satire, Fielding identifies himself with both Swift and Hogarth. His targets were cultural rather than political. Signing himself Lemuel Gulliver 'Poet Laureat to the King of Lilliput', he published a long poem *The Masquerade*, tackling a common subject of 1720s satire, depicted vividly, for example, in Hogarth's 1724 print, *Masquerades and Operas*. Like Hogarth, Fielding pokes fun at John James Heidegger, a Swiss impresario whose vast, elaborate, masked assemblies at the Opera House in the Haymarket were attacked by clergy as 'scandalous'. Fielding's narrator attends the masquerade disguised as a poor poet and hits all the standard evils: vanity, gossip, coquetry, the triviality of current taste. The scene is liberating, frenetic, risky, and sexy ('Thus Fortune sends the gamesters luck, / Venus her votary a ——' (*FH* XIV. 343–4)), but the masquerade also invokes doubleness, hypocrisy, and entrapment. Disorder as well as fun rules this world turned upside down.

> As in a madman's frantic skull,
> When pale-fac'd Luna is at full,
> In wild confusion huddled lies
> A heap of incoherencies:
> So here in one confusion hurl'd,
> Seem all the nations of the world;
> Cardinals, quakers, judges dance;
> Grim Turks are coy, and nuns advance.
> Grave churchmen here at hazard play;
> Cinque-ace ten pound – done, quater-tray.
> Known prudes there, libertines we find,
> Who masque the face, t'unmasque the mind.

(*FH* VII. ll. 63–74)

His first play, *Love in Several Masques*, also takes up the theme of disguise. It was performed at the Theatre-Royal, Drury Lane, on 16 February 1728, just before his twenty-first birthday, a startling and prestigious début for someone so young. A common lament of the day was the impossibility of getting plays accepted by Drury Lane's managers, Colley Cibber and John Wilks, unless you were backed by powerful 'Interest': Fielding's luck was undoubtedly due to the influence of Mary Wortley Montagu, to whom the play was dedicated, and Anne Oldfield, who played the part of Lady Matchless. He did not achieve a triumph, but he didn't let them down: his own escapade at Lyme provided a skeleton plot and, while the intrigue is conventional, the variations on stock Restoration characters (like the oafish squire 'Sir Positive Trap', or the fop, 'Lord Formal') showed an early skill with conventions.

Rather surprisingly, Fielding then turned his back on London for eighteen months, enrolling as a student of letters (classical studies) at the University of Leiden, until he ran out of cash and fled, leaving belongings, books, and creditors behind. At this juncture, Mary Wortley Montagu remembered him saying, he felt he had to choose between being 'a Hackney Writer or a Hackney Coachman'.[2] In the next ten years he wrote over twenty plays: by the age of 24 he was the most talked-about playwright in London. In 1734 he married Charlotte Cradock, from Salisbury, and brought her back to their cramped lodgings off the Strand, in the parish of St Martins in the Fields. Except for a few months in East Stour in 1735, this square mile of London would always be Fielding's base.

2

Luckless, the central figure in *The Author's Farce*, Fielding's first great theatrical hit in 1730, is a young dramatist. He owes money to his landlady Mrs Moneywood; she makes advances to him; he loves her daughter Harriot. First his play is rejected by the publisher Bookweight, who keeps a stable of hacks writing pamphlets, inventing murders for the papers (plus ghosts) and providing classical mottoes (sixpence for Latin, threepence for Greek — the latter is easier since no one understands it anyway). Next, Luckless is turned down by the all-powerful Marplay and Sparkish (Colley Cibber and Wilks); behind the scenes the two managers confer:

SPARKISH. What dost think of the play?
MARPLAY. It may be a very good one for aught I know; but I know the author has no interest.
SPARKISH. Give me interest and rat the play.

(*AF* II. ii)

In desperation, lacking influence and knowing the taste of the day, Luckless puts on an old puppet-play, *The Pleasures of the Town*, using actors as puppets, mixing Punch and Judy with scenes at the court of the Goddess of Nonsense, across the Styx, featuring quarrelling cultural figures – Don Tragedio (Lewis Theobald), Sir Farcical Comic (Colley Cibber), Dr Orator (John Henley), Signior Opera (Francesco Senesino), Monsieur Panto-mime (John Rich), and Mrs Novel (Eliza Haywood). The play narrowly escapes being closed by the killjoy Presbyterian, Murdertext, before the action swells to a riotous conclusion, as hectic messengers announce that Luckless is first the Prince, then the King, of Bantam (realm of exotic wealth). Suddenly 'real life' and fantasy start to swamp each other. All the puppets receive posts of honour at the Bantomite court and everyone is found to be related to everyone else, puppets included: Punch reveals that Mrs Moneywood is not only the Queen of Old Brentford (wife of one of the Kings of Brentford in Buckingham's *The Rehearsal*), but is, moreover, his mother. Joyful reunions follow:

MONEYWOOD. Oh, my son!
HARRIOT. Oh, my brother!
PUNCH. Oh, my sister!
MONEYWOOD. I am sorry, in this pickle, to remember who I am. But, alas, too true is all you've said.

(*AF* III. i)

'True' is the crux. In this parodic discovery scene, art, artifice, and reality cannot be untangled, for Luckless himself is a character in a play, quite as unreal and 'emblematical' as the one he has written; his own genealogy is theatrical. Furthermore, as in Fielding's other 'rehearsal plays' (one of his favourite dramatic frames), the 'actors' in the play-within-a–play are given a rich off-stage as well as a double on-stage life – failing to turn up because they have lost their gloves, are drunk, have to meet someone: yet we know that even this unseen, third-remove life is fictional too.

Fielding may have taken the rehearsal frame from Buckingham, the interleaved songs from Gay, the Dulness motif from Pope, and the Dialogue of the Dead from Lucian, but the ebullient use of genre is all his own. Not until Pirandello and Brecht, Alfred Jarry and Genet, do we find such obsessive, self-aware dramatization of the theory and practice of 'enactment', linked to hard-hitting satire. The possibilities of reflection and multiple reference are endless. A coda to *The Author's Farce*, 'Punch's Oratory: Or, The Pleasures of the Town', was acted separately that summer, as a puppet-play at Reynolds's Great Theatrical Booth in Tottenham Court. The advertisement ended 'No Wires, all alive'. The joke is good, but the point is serious, for someone *is* pulling those wires – and where, then, is 'truth' to be found?

The plays are a revelation to those who first come to Fielding through his novels: in their pace, their linguistic and formal play, dizzying overlay of references, fierce moral and political stands – and sometimes their sheer silliness. His return from Leiden coincided with a boom in the London theatre: new theatres sprang up alongside the official 'patent' theatres like the Theatre-Royal in Drury Lane, and sometimes five or six plays were showing on one day. The mood was flamboyant and experimental: increasingly, 'irregular' plays were added as 'afterpieces' to the 'regular' five-act comedy or tragedy – a farce, a pantomime, or (following the success of *The Beggar's Opera* in 1728) a 'ballad opera' with satirical content, packed with new songs set to well-known tunes.

Fielding began with a conventional five-act comedy of intrigue, *The Temple Beau*, but it was in the irregular form that he really flourished, starting with *The Author's Farce* in March 1730. For this play, rebuffed by the principal theatres, he had turned to the 'Little Theatre' in the Haymarket, a makeshift, informal playhouse with keen, if inexperienced, actors. That April, hot on the heels of *The Author's Farce*, the Little Theatre staged *Tom Thumb*, a mock-heroic diminution of the 'Great Man', Walpole, in which chap-book characters declaim with bombast and bathos, and the giant-killing Tom, brandishing his sword, proves that Size is not All – or so his Epilogue suggests:

> But, for the Ladies, they, I know despise
> The little Things of my inferior Size.
> Their mighty Souls are all of them too large

To take so small a Heroe to their Charge.
Take Pity, Ladies, on a young beginner;
Faith! I may prove, in time, a thumping Sinner.

(*TT.* Epilogue)

The urgent zest of this little hero is hard to resist – Swift allegedly laughed aloud when the ghost of Tom Thumb was killed, one of two recorded occasions in his life – and the tragic lamentations of Princess Huncamunca would echo through the ages as far as Beatrix Potter's *Two Bad Mice*, the nursery tale come full circle.

Only a month after this triumph, separated by Fielding's serious Jacobean humour play, *Rape upon Rape*, came a third hit, *The Welsh Opera*. A scandalous satire, packed with tuneful songs, it was revised the following year as *The Grub-Street Opera*, but suppressed (perhaps by Fielding himself) before it was staged or published. At the same time, in the face of government harrassment of the Little Theatre, Fielding moved to Drury Lane. There, over the next four years, he staged farces such as *The Lottery* and *The Intriguing Chambermaid*, five-act comedies like *The Modern Husband*, and translations (or adaptations) of Molière, *The Mock Doctor* and *The Miser*. But in 1736 he and his friend John Ralph took over the Little Theatre entirely with his own troupe 'The Great Mogul's Company of Comedians', made up of young actors from Drury Lane. Over the next year came a flurry of irregular plays, including the tumultuously acclaimed 'rehearsal plays' *Pasquin* and *The Historical Register for the Year 1736*. (It is no problem says the playwright Medley, to fit the political and cultural events of a year into half an hour, since nothing of note has happened.) *The Historical Register* almost broke dramatic form with its plotless mosaic of walk-on scenes. It also shattered Fielding's career. The portrayal of Walpole as the fiddler Quidam, bribing the patriots, making them dance to his tune, and scooping back the money as it falls from their pockets, finally spurred the government into passing the Theatre Licensing Act of 1737, which restricted the number of theatres to those with official patents, and required all new plays to be licensed by the Lord Chamberlain. 'Mr Fielding's Scandal Shop', as Eliza Haywood called it, was closed. An urge to attack had fired his plays. Barred from the fray, he withdrew to study law (to the hilarity of his enemies) until the publication of Richardson's *Pamela* roused his ire and ridicule again.

Critics differ about Fielding's plays, some thinking time merciful in consigning them to dusty library shelves, others lamenting their oblivion. Occasionally a passionate admirer surfaces, like George Bernard Shaw, who thought Fielding the greatest dramatist, bar Shakespeare, between the Middle Ages and the twentieth century. The reason they faded from literary and stage history is the reason for their success – their topicality. At the time, this was an advantage, since Fielding could revise them to take in new events, or alter them on publication, adding deadpan dedications, like that of *The Welsh Opera* to Walpole, or of *The Historical Register* to the 'Town'. (How could the Ministry think he was depicting them, he asks, when his politicians are such obvious blockheads?) The wildest textual addition is the spoof editorial apparatus attached to *The Tragedy of Tragedies* (like Pope's *Dunciad Variorum* of 1729), a hopeless proliferation of notes by 'Scriblerus Secundus', giving dates, defining 'giants', solemnly tracing classical allusions, and obtusely misreading the entire play.

On stage, however, the full flavour of the comedy demands an audience who share the context and who can grasp a reference almost before it is given, or where it is so familiar – as in much of the satire on Walpole – that it need not be made explicit at all. The layering of allusions to hit multiple targets assumes intimate understanding of forms and styles as well as topics and personalities. (Modern British television satire from *Monty Python* to *Spitting Image* uses similar techniques – imagine a sketch, say, where soap-opera stars sing a rock ballad about Jean-Paul Sartre, in a bank vault, during the World Cup). It is easy to forget what a small world the London theatre-goers of the 1730s belonged to: they knew each other; they knew all the theatrical personalities and followed their scandals and family squabbles. They knew the court; they knew the City; they rushed to fashionable auctions like those run by Christopher Cock; they saw all the new shows – sometimes three or four times – and could recognize a caricature in a gesture or the twist of an eyebrow. The private lives of 'the Great' were such a subject of gossip – whether it was Walpole's affair with Molly Skerrett, or Queen Caroline's influence over George II, or their son Prince Frederick's rumoured impotence – that a playwright only had to depict a parallel situation for everyone to get the point. This is exactly what Fielding does in *The Welsh Opera*, where Squire

Apshinken is ruled by his mean-spirited, religious wife, his son Owen flirts feebly with the maids, and the mercenary butler, Robin, rules the household. So hidden are the slanderous, even treasonable, allusions that the play can be read simply as a rollicking provincial, Farquhar-like comedy. Surfaces deceive.

The leading analogy in Fielding's day – in books, poems, pamphlets, and plays – was between the stage and politics: thus a caricature of a theatrical leader is automatically a political jibe too, as Medley explains in *The Historical Register*:

> When my politics come to a farce, they very naturally lead to the playhouse where, let me tell you, there are some politicians too, where there is lying, flattering, dissembling, promising, deceiving and undermining, as well as in any court in Christendom. (*HR* I. i)

Actors may be as useless and cynical as politicians, he adds later, but 'though the audience damn both, yet while they both receive their pay, they laugh at the public behind the scenes'. The playhouse could act as a metaphor for general society too, as it was frequented by all classes: aristocrat and merchant, pimp and pickpocket. Fielding's own characters are always dashing off to the playhouse, missing the first act, or not knowing the name of the play. He was writing about, as well as addressing, his mixed audience, and made the most of the opportunity, linking boxes and pit, high life and low. *The Covent-Garden Tragedy*, a ribald burlesque of Ambrose Philips's neoclassical *The Distrest Mother*, replaces Philips's heroine, Andromache, by the brothel-keeper Mother Punchbowl (the notorious Mother Needham, a real bawd, caricatured in Hogarth's series of prints, *The Harlot's Progress* in 1731). The tongue-in-cheek prologue explains that the didactic dramatist has turned from Greece and Rome to bring a 'curious draft of tragic nectar'.

> From Covent Garden culls delicious stores
> Of bullies, bawds and sots, and rakes, and whores.
> Examples of the great can serve but few;
> For what are kings' and heroes' faults to you?
> But these examples are of general use.
> What rake is ignorant of King's Coffee-house?
>
> (*CGT* Prologue)

One world can stand for another. All that differs are clothes and language.

Language is the stuff of Fielding's art and he defends it passionately. Many of his plays contrast the popular Italian opera and non-verbal buffoonery of rope-dancers, fire-eaters, and pantomime with the richness of 'true' drama. In the current theatre, as Trapwit's comedy in *Pasquin* shows, language is in danger of extinction:

> TRAPWIT. I must desire a strict silence through this whole scene. Colonel, stand you still on this side of the stage; and miss, do you stand on the opposite. – There, now look at each other. [*A long silence here*].
>
> FUSTIAN. Pray, Mr Trapwit, is nobody ever to speak again?
>
> TRAPWIT. Oh! The devil! You have interrupted the scene; after all my precautions the scene's destroyed; the best scene of silence that ever was penned by man.

(P. III. i)

But words can be as empty as silence, like the bombast of *Tom Thumb*, with its riot of absurd epic similes and overblown outbursts: 'Confusion, Horror, Murder, Guts and Death' (*TT* II. vii). Many of the most ludicrous lines in this play were wickedly pinched from contemporary plays. In Fielding's view, tragedy was devaluing feeling, and in the Prologue to *The Author's Farce* a slick rhyme shows how words which should have real value have become stage and party slogans:

> Or when in armor of Corinthian brass
> Heroic actor stares you in the face,
> And cries aloud, with emphasis that's fit, on
> Liberty, freedom, liberty and Briton.

(AF Prologue)

The same play shows how language can be rendered senseless by neologisms as well as repetition, in the heroic over-kill of Don Tragedio who 'does not only glean up all the bad words of other authors but makes new bad words of his own' (*AF* III. i).

Wit, the traditional sparring tool of Restoration comedy, can also deny meaning. Introducing *The Grub-Street Opera*, Scriblerus (who can be acute as well as obtuse) declares, 'Ah, ah, the whole wit of Grub Street consists in these two little words – *you lie*' (*GSO* Introduction). (Grub Street, near Moorfields, was traditionally the home of poor authors, and became a synonym for hack writing of all kinds.) And in *Pasquin*, as Trapwit yet again unwittingly betrays his empty hand, Fielding hits out at contemporary plays, including his own. 'Mr Fustian', says Trapwit,

> you'll observe I do not begin this play like most of our modern comedies, with three or four gentlemen who are brought on only to talk wit: for to tell you the truth, Sir, I have very little, if any wit in this play: No, Sir, this is a play consisting of humour, nature, and simplicity: It is written, Sir, in the exact and true spirit of Molière; and this I will say for it, that except about a dozen, or a score or so, there is not one impure joke in it. (P. I. i)

The ideal of 'humour, nature and simplicity', travestied here, would be Fielding's own aim as a novelist.

Within the plays, simple tricks show how language can itself become corrupt, the form of words laying a veneer of 'gentility' over baser feelings and motivations. This is neatly demonstrated by Punch and Judy's song in 'The Pleasures of the Town':

PUNCH.	Joan, you are the plague of my life.
	A rope would be welcomer than such a wife.
JOAN.	Punch, your merits had you but shared,
	Your neck had been longer by half a yard.
PUNCH.	Ugly witch.
JOAN.	Son of a bitch.
BOTH.	Would you were hanged or drowned in a ditch.

Here they dance again.

PUNCH.	Since we hate, like people in vogue,
	Let us call not bitch and rogue.
	Gentler titles let us use,
	Hate each other, but not abuse.
JOAN.	Pretty dear!
PUNCH.	Ah! ma chère!
BOTH.	Joy of my life and only care.

(*AF* III. iii)

The linguistic swerves of marital hostility anticipate the magnificent rows between Jonathan Wild and Laetitia; in the novel, as in the song, language itself is an actor. The same direct agency is given to rhetoric, jargon, and 'authority', often a bluff for ignorance, as in the doctors' speeches in *Tom Thumb* ('a Distemper which *Paracelsus* calls the *Diaphormane*, *Hippocrates* the *Caetecumen*, *Galen* the *Regon*' (*TT* II. vi)), or in the even richer nonsense of Gregory in *The Mock Doctor*:

Besides, sir, certain spirits passing from the left side, which is the seat of the liver, to the right, which is the seat of the heart, we find the lungs, which we call in Latin, Whiskerus, having communication with the brain, which we name in Greek, Jackbootos, by means of a hollow vein, which we call in Hebrew, Periwiggus, meet in the road with the said spirits which fill the ventricles of the Omotoplasmus. (*MD* I. ix)

When the bewildered Sir Jasper says he thought the heart was on the left, and the liver on the right, Gregory swiftly finds an answer: 'Ay, sir, so they were formerly; but we have changed all that. The college at present, sir, proceeds upon an entire new method.' 'I ask your pardon, sir,' says Sir Jasper meekly.

Fielding is enjoying himself hugely, but his point is not so much that such language is funny as that it makes things happen: it is an active force. Of all the Fielding plays, the Molière adaptations show this most clearly, because here the characters have an appealing complexity and vulnerability, which lets them almost leap free of the conventions – as they often do in the novels. The scene in *The Miser* where the maid Lappet slowly twists Lovegold towards the idea of marrying Mariana, by appealing to his vanity and his purse, gradually building his excitement to a peak, is a *tour de force* of linguistic–sexual seduction. We seem to see her words operating, spinning like a top, in a whirl of greed, lust, and casuistry.

Language is dangerous, whether it be an active weapon, as in *The Miser*, or the more insidious clothing of a cast of mind. Sometimes the joke is on us: we laugh at King Arthur's speech, when he hears that Tom Thumb has been swallowed by a cow.

> Shut up again the Prisons, bid my Treasurer
> Not give three Farthings out – hang all the *Culprits*,
> Guilty or not – no matter. – Ravish Virgins,
> Go bid the School-masters whip all their Boys;
> Let Lawyers, Parsons and Physicians loose,
> To rob, impose on, and to kill the world.

(*TT* III. x)

But in the hands of real tyrants, Fielding hints, such ludicrous heroic language validates despotism, absolute power triggered by petty rage. It is the author's duty to make us face unpalatable political truths by rendering the rhetoric so absurd that we literally 'see through it'.

Fielding wrote to make money, spent it as soon as he got it, and therefore had to write more. He may not have worked as fast as his character Pillage, who writes 'nine scenes with spirit in a day', but his first biographer, Arthur Murphy, describes him writing on scraps of tobacco-paper late at night after an evening in the tavern – and some of his scenes do have a quality of heady improvisation. But although he needed to divert the town, he also wrote with a deeper purpose. In the letter to the actress Kitty Clive which prefaces *The Intriguing Chambermaid*, he asserts that, 'while I hold the pen, it will be a maxim with me, that vice can never be too great to be lashed, nor virtue too obscure to be commended; in other words that satire can never rise too high, nor panegyrick stoop too low' (*IT*, Preface).

Satire, however, can become reductive, eating its own tail. In *The Historical Register*, one can feel Fielding chafing, mocking the littleness of satire itself, so familiar that even actors could write it.

> FIRST PLAYER. ... 'gad, I fancy I could write a thing to succeed, myself.
> SECOND PLAYER. Ay, prithee, what subject wouldst thou write on?
> FIRST PLAYER. Why no subject at all, sir, but I would have a humming deal of satire, and I would repeat in every page that courtiers are cheats and don't pay their debts, that lawyers are rogues, physicians blockheads, soldiers cowards, and ministers...
> SECOND PLAYER. Well, what sir?
> FIRST PLAYER. Nay, I'll only name 'em, that's enough to set the audience a-hooting.

> (*HR* I. i)

Who needs a playwright?

In *Eurydice Hiss'd*, the afterpiece to the *Register*, Fielding satirizes himself and Walpole together, an astonishing piece of self-denigration. This brief play traces the downfall of Pillage, 'the author of a mighty farce at the very top and pinnacle of poetical or rather farcical greatness' (*EH* I. i). It is as if Fielding has realized that if politics are constantly presented as ridiculous they lose meaning. We begin to accept government as game; as a child's story, like *Tom Thumb*, or a nursery-rhyme world, like *The Grub-Street Opera*. Attacking, self-referential comedy can become over-cynical and solipsistic. Fielding's inventive exuberance saves him, but he still faces the problem that, within satire, it is far harder to commend virtue than to lash vice. The opposing good is always seen as weak, or absent, like Queen Common-sense facing the armies of ignorance in *Pasquin*, or like the commodities no one bids for in the auction in *The Historical Register*: Modesty, Common-sense, Conscience. The most persuasive figure of virtue in his drama is, in every sense, a misfit, borrowed from a different genre. When *Don Quixote in England* was staged in 1733, the fantastical Spaniard, clinging to his knightly ideals, falls, uncomprehending, into the middle of a British village election. To those around him Quixote's words make no sense at all, yet it is he who points to the gap between the words and the actions of the squire, parson, and Lord and eventually proves them 'all to be more mad than himself' (*DQE* III. xvi).

Fielding's positive beliefs would find expression in the wider canvas, slower movement, and greater flexibility of fiction, but his plays paved the way. The insistent but deceptive narrators, the layered metaphors, the non-realistic representation of character, the exuberant rhetoric, the rapid build-up of action, and the technique of diminishing 'the Great' found their way into his novels, and so, too, did the benign essence of Quixote. Despite his delusions, Quixote is true to his ideals: because of this integrity – however mad – he is able to make others see themselves as they are. Truth lies beyond logic and 'realism'. Besieged by a society ruled by self-interest, the Don embodies active good-nature – the most characteristic of all Fielding virtues, which will also govern those other erring, life-bringing heroes, Abraham Adams, and Tom Jones.

2

Towards Fiction: The *Champion* and *Shamela*

1

After the Licensing Act, Fielding had no recourse if he was to feed his family – he now had two children – but to revert to the sober Gould tradition. In November 1737 he entered the Middle Temple: in June 1740 he was called to the Bar. For the next few years he was a barrister in Assize Courts, travelling on the Western Circuit – Cornwall, Devon, Somerset, Dorset, and Hampshire. His rapid start was helped by his uncle, Sir Davidge Gould, a Master of the Bench at the Temple, but he still packed the legal training of several years into two and a half, tackling the law with the same energy as he had play-writing. His friends remembered that he would come back late to his chambers after a heavy night out 'and there read, and make extracts from, the most abstruse authors, for several hours before he went to bed'.[1]

Family life did not put a stop to taverns and coffee-houses or indeed, to Grub Street hack-work, essential to his income. But all his literary work, leading up to his assault on Samuel Richardson in *Shamela*, was still in some way concerned with the language, form, and morality, and with the way individuals developed a particular 'persona' which disguised their essential character and interests. In the terrible winter of 1739–40, for example, he agreed to translate the three volume *Military History of Charles XII King of Sweden* by Gustave Adlerfeld (already translated from Swedish into French). His plight was that of Mr Wilson in *Joseph Andrews*, who has to accept translating work for a pittance and is given so much 'that in half a year I almost writ myself blind' (*JA/S* 194), but the task was not without interest. The life of the fiery, despotic Charles XII (1682–1718) fascinated authors from Voltaire and Defoe to Samuel Johnson. Voltaire saw him as a man whose good qualities became vices because taken to excess: to Fielding, as a type of modern Alexander, he was another example of dangerous imbalance and self-obsessed 'Greatness'. It is no coincidence that his early work on *Jonathan Wild* dates from this period.

Another literary experiment was a newspaper, the *Champion*, launched in November 1739 in collaboration with James Ralph. By mid-1740 Fielding had virtually left editorial control to Ralph, but still wrote for the paper, shuffling his articles under legal briefs when clients arrived. He had planned to write on social and literary topics rather than politics, since the Opposition already had two papers, *Common Sense* and the *Craftsman*. Although politics was what people wanted and, as sales dipped, the *Champion* adjusted accordingly, Fielding's own contributions usually dealt with private attitudes and excesses rather than public policy.

The *Champion* was published three times a week, expanding after a few months from two to four pages. The first page was usually an essay by Fielding, sometimes followed by a 'Literary Article' and then by a satiric digest of foreign and domestic news. Although he was new to the genre, Fielding quickly imposed his own style. As a mouthpiece, he followed Addison's creation of Sir Roger de Coverley in the *Spectator*. But, typically, he adopted a more demotic voice, appearing as the ex-prize-fighter 'Captain Hercules Vinegar of Hockley in the Hole' (an arena and beargarden near Clerkenwell Green). Taking up his cudgels, Captain Vinegar summons his family – his scolding wife, Joan (to represent the concerns of the fairer sex), father, Nehemiah (for politics), a lawyer uncle, a doctor cousin, a classical scholar brother, and two sons, law student Tom (theatre) and idle Jack (gossip). Advised by this clan, the Captain holds his own court, to try not murderers but those who destroy lives in subtler ways: 'the Covetous, the Prodigal, the Bully, the Vain, the Hypocrite, the Flatterer, the Slanderer, call aloud for the Champion's Vengeance' (C. 113). Since the English love executions, punishments will take place on Drury Lane stage (in the intervals) and, though he will not hang anyone, he will 'deal with them in such a Manner, that it may be presumed they will hang themselves' (C. 115).

The Vinegar persona lets Fielding be fierce without being solemn. The Captain's world-view is not always consistent; sometimes he attacks misanthropists, proposing the Augustan ideals of harmony and 'Nature' as standards which can be reclaimed; sometimes he seems to hold a Hobbesian view of man's innate depravity, recalling Pope's elemental rule of Dullness:

> Laborious, heavy, busy, bold and blind,
> She rul'd in native Anarchy, the Mind.[2]

The dread of anarchy lies behind his attack on atheism, for example, since, without fear in God and an afterlife, he argues, mankind might 'pursue their Desires, their Appetites, their Lusts, in a full Swing, without Control' (C. 164).

Such anarchy can be controlled by customs of behaviour as well as spiritual and moral principles, and many of Fielding's essays return to the concept of 'good-breeding' (a social, not biological, term, which cuts across classes, but still keeps a tang of aristocratic superiority). The problem here, constantly rephrased in his fiction, is that the manners essential to civilized relations may also provide a disguise for hypocrites to entrap the innocent. The real means of control must lie within, and the essays stress the importance of 'good-nature', the ability to realize the needs of others as vividly as one's own desires. This Shaftesburian term is not unique to Fielding, but his definition gives it a particularly firm expression:

Good-nature is a delight in the Happiness of Mankind, and a Concern at their Misery, with a Desire, as much as possible, to procure the former, and avert the latter, and this, with a constant Regard to Desert....

This makes us gentle without Fear, humble without Hopes, and charitable without Ostentation, and extends the Power, Knowledge, Strength and Riches of the Individual to the Good of the Whole.

(C. 258, 259)

Fielding's ideal is a rigorous, practical goodness, springing from sympathy, tempered by a critical awareness of self and others. Any imbalance or excess which distorts judgement will impose false values and thereby ultimately damage the social fabric. This is true in all fields, in scholarship as much as politics, but especially within influential institutions of government, law, or religion.

Politicians and lawyers would later be pilloried in Fielding's novels, but it is the clergy – Parson Williams in *Shamela*, Barnabas and Trulliber in *Joseph Andrews*, Thwackum in *Tom Jones* – who often seem most dangerous, their shared weakness being the placing of doctrine before acts, and the gulf between the abstractions they mouth – grace, mercy, justice – and their selfish behaviour. Fielding was no Deist or Materialist, although (again like Mr Wilson) he had associated with free-thinking groups in his youth, but his religion is social rather than spiritual. His *Champion* articles, 'An Apology for the Clergy', emphasize the parson's pastoral role, and when he did create a model clergyman, in Abraham Adams, it is his charity that he stresses.

Adams's superficial absurdities, however fondly treated, illustrate another deep-held belief: that excess can make even good qualities ridiculous: 'It will be found, I believe, a pretty just Observation, that more Vices and Follies arrive in the World through Excess than Neglect. Passion hurries ten beyond the Mark, for one whom Indolence holds short of it' (C. 243). Even modesty, if exaggerated, can become prudery and affectation, 'and make a Woman, what Sir Richard Steele calls *outragiously virtuous*'. But the mean is hard to hold, and vice and virtue appear perilously close: 'Covetousness and Thrift, Profuseness and Liberality, Cowardice and Caution, Rashness and Bravery, Praise and Adulation have been all very often mistaken for one another' (C. 229). The author must expose the false and display the true.

Comedy is the natural mode for such teaching, since, in Fielding's view, we laugh first at things which are imbalanced: at figures at odds with their surroundings; actions out of kilter with statements. In the *Champion*'s studies of misleading appearance or the folly of fame, in the 'type' portraits – the Flatterer, the Hypocrite, the Miser – or in the clever letters from invented readers, one sees the novelist emerging. Even the more abstract definitions of terms – Virtue, Valour and Wit, Authority – will reappear in the novels, dramatized through conflicts of character. Thus, in the discussion of mercy in *Tom Jones*, Tom has the 'amiable Quality of Mercy', while Blifil holds out for Justice, a 'higher' virtue learnt from Thwackum and Square:

for though they would both make frequent Use of the Word *Mercy*, yet it was plain, that in reality Square held it to be inconsistent with the Rule of Right; and Thwackum was for doing Justice, and leaving Mercy to Heaven. The two Gentlemen did indeed somewhat differ in Opinion concerning the Objects of this sublime Virtue; by which Thwackum would probably have destroyed one half of Mankind, and Square the other half. (*TJ* 147)

The fiction, however, also draws its vitality from the very excess that Fielding castigates – despite himself, he warms to the unruly, the unpredictable, the extreme. His praise of moderation often has a rather wistful tone, as in his insistence that, because he conserves his energies, 'the temperate Man tastes and relishes Pleasure in a Degree infinitely superior to that of the voluptuous' (*C.* 167). The essays look forward to *Tom Jones* and *Amelia* as much as to *Joseph Andrews* in Fielding's description of self-control as a continuing battle for the individual man: 'an army of obstinate Passions that will hold him in tight play, will often force his Reason to retreat' (*C.* 177). In particular, he inveighs bitterly against imprisonment for debt, admitting that he looks on 'Indiscretion with Pity, not Abhorrence, and on no Indiscretion with so much Pity as Extravagance', which 'may bring Men into the greatest Calamities of this life' (*C.* 206).

Debt certainly brought pressure, if not calamity, on Fielding himself. Attacker of corruption though he was, his political principles did, on occasion, succumb to his personal needs. He was not immune to the gilded persuasions of Walpole. In October 1740 he wrote a satire featuring a quack doctor who offers golden pills to a hostile writer: a hundred to 'stay at Home and be quiet and neuter', two hundred to 'say a *single word* in my favour', and, if he will, 'declaim handsomely upon my Nostrums', three hundred, 'besides something very good to take twice a Year'.[3] In this piece Fielding admitted he had already suppressed one book (most possibly the draft of *Jonathan Wild*) and six months later he would produce a pro-Walpole poem 'The Opposition: A Vision', in which his erstwhile colleagues are shown as a hopelessly disorganized bunch, their coach stuck in the mire, forced to hitch it to the ministerial wagon. But as his fortunes recovered his politics swung back, and he lambasted the government again in January 1741 with his satiric poem *The Vernoniad*, about the catastrophic campaign in the West Indies.

Despite these swerves and prevarications, there is no doubt that Fielding's sympathies were, throughout, still with the 'Patriot' opposition. This group, who included his Eton schoolmates George Lyttleton and William Pitt, had been joined in 1739 by George Bubb Dodington. Lyttleton and Dodington were Fielding's lifelong supporters, and he praised the latter in his poem 'Of True Greatness' for his dignity and integrity – and his generosity.

He had need of such generous patrons. His debts, as well as his writings, had made him notorious. In late 1740 his creditors gathered, and in March 1741 he was detained in a bailiff's sponging-house, the last stop before debtor's prison. There, in the fortnight before he was bailed, he dashed off a little work that spun all the *Champion*'s themes of hypocrisy, false religion, and linguistic laxness into a new and hilarious shape: *An Apology for the Life of Mrs Shamela Andrews*, by 'Conny Keyber'.

2

Shamela was prompted by three books that had made Fielding's blood boil in 1740. The most important was Samuel Richardson's *Pamela*, in which, through her plangent, urgent letters home, we follow the young servant's brave attempts to foil the assaults on her virtue by her master, Mr B——, (including kidnapping, near-rape, and virtual imprisonment), until the final resolution in a happy marriage and handsome settlement. Fielding thought the novel an example of bad morality and (almost a worse sin) bad writing, and was outraged by its rapturous reception, especially by the clergy.

A second source of irritation was *An Apology for the Life of Colley Cibber, Comedian, Written by Himself*, published in March 1740. The book's flatulent self-esteem, grammatical scrambling, and mis-used words (surely a source for Mrs Slipslop's errors in *Joseph Andrews*), had provoked some of the funniest *Champion* articles, culminating in Cibber's inglorious trial for 'Assault on the English Language'. The self-congratulatory tone and bubbling, incon-sequential style seep brilliantly into the text of *Shamela*, which nods openly to Cibber through its coy title and phoney author (Keyber being the original Dutch form of Cibber).

The 'Conny' of 'Conny Keyber' immediately suggests a hoax

(through 'coney', a gull or dupe) and a bawdy read (through 'cunny'). But it also points to a third target, Conyers Middleton, Fellow of Trinity College Cambridge and author of a new life of Cicero. Fielding thought Middleton's book terrible, but what really made him laugh was its obsequious dedication to Lord Hervey, Walpole's Privy Seal. The 'Dedication' in *Shamela* is an open parody, adopting Pope's name for the effeminate Hervey 'Miss Fanny', and making each of Middleton's grovelling phrases ridiculous (and usually sexual): Middleton's boast that 'some Parts of my present Work have been brightened by the Strokes of your Lordship's Pencil' becomes 'Madam, I must tell the World that you have tickled up and brightened many Strokes in this Work by your Pencil', while his admiration at finding Hervey 'engaged with the Classical writers' on early morning visits becomes a dawn assignation, 'when I have constantly found you reading in good Books; and if ever I have drawn you upon me, I have always felt you very heavy' (*JA/S* 317).

Much of this, like *Shamela* itself, is pure foolery, but the political sting is noticeable. It is amplified in the 'Letters to the Editor' (imitating the rapturous letters Richardson inserted in the second edition of *Pamela* and quoting many of the more ludicrous phrases), when Fielding's 'John Puff' suggests that the creator of Parson Williams might move on to a life of '*his honour*' (Walpole) since there is 'little more to do than pull off the Parson's Gown ... and the Cap will Fit' (*JA/S* 319). In the framing of Shamela, politics and letters are thus undermined as purveyors of false standards, while a similar moral blindness within the church is suggested by Parson Tickletext, who hotly recommends *Pamela* (but cannot help reverting always to the 'emotion' he feels, and even dreams of, on thinking of her sexual trials). In reaction, Parson Oliver (named after Fielding's boyhood tutor) is appalled that families can recommend such scenes to their daughters and horrified that the public should be hoodwinked by self-interest masked as virtue. His anger, and Fielding's, prompts these 'authentic' letters, exposing Pamela's sham.

The religious, literary, and political allusions made Fielding's burlesque topical and deepened its resonance. Like his plays-within-a-play, *Shamela* is a book within a book: an exposure of the overall culture of 'acting', as well as a wicked parody of writing. The way books are puffed mirrors the way actions and fundamental attitudes are misread. Fielding's strategy in the main text is simple and clever. First, (as in *The Covent-Garden Tragedy*) he transposes the early action from the country to Drury Lane and turns Richardson's good characters into guilty ones: Shamela from reluctant prey to eager predator, her mother from naïve peasant to knowing bawd, Mrs Jervis from kindly housekeeper to professional procuress. The effect is to introduce us to a world where bodies are openly, rather than covertly, for sale. The use of other correspondents (Shamela's mother, Mrs Jervis, Parson Williams) places Shamela's action in perspective, and also allows Fielding to summarize (and ridicule) the plot. Shamela's own letters can thus concentrate on crises, their style mocking all Richardson's mannerisms. One such mannerism is the apparently naïve spontaneity – and therefore authenticity – of recording events as they occur, the trick of the 'writing for the moment':

> *Thursday Night, Twelve o'Clock*
> Mrs. Jervis, and I are just in Bed, and the Door unlocked; if my Master should come – Odsbobs! I hear him just coming in at the Door. You see I write in the present Tense, as Parson *Williams* says... (*JA/S* 330)

Through such mimicry and compression Fielding catches the underlying tone of Richardson's prose, whether it be the heated immediacy, the prurience of his semi-sadistic seduction scenes, or the bourgeois stress on money, property, and manners.

> Mrs. *Jewkes* went in with me, and helped me to pack up my little All, which was soon done; being no more than two Day-Caps, two Night-Caps, five Shifts, one Sham, a Hoop, a Quilted-Petticoat, two Flannel-Petticoats, two pair of Stockings, one odd one, a pair of lac'd Shoes, a short flowered Apron, a lac'd Neck-Handkerchief, one Clog, and almost another, and some few books: as *A full Answer to a plain and true Account* &c., *The Whole Duty of Man*, with only the Duty to one's Neighbour, torn out. The Third Volume of the *Atlantis. Venus in the Cloyster: Or, the Nun in her Smock. God's Dealings with Mr. Whitefield. Orfus and Eurydice.* Some Sermon-Books; and two or three Plays, with their titles and Part of the first Act torn off. (*JA/S* 344).

As Shamela literally crams everything in, Fielding caricatures the way Pamela's piety and fainting timidity never quite overwhelm her avid interest in dress, or her stylistic passion for detail. Fielding descends to joyful spoof ('one Clog, and almost another') but he also makes a serious point about the 'authorities' which ballast her physical and moral luggage. She mingles her mangled plays and pornography, with popular religious tracts 'with the Duty to one's Neighbour torn out', and the works of the Methodist George Whitefield, whose *'Dealings'* appeared in 1740. Fielding detested Methodist enthusiasm, which set the self-dramatizing individual spirit above the needs of the community (men wept and rolled on the ground in misery at their sins, at Whitefield's huge outdoor meetings). But in his eyes both Whitefield and his complacent Anglican opponent Joseph Trapp were equally guilty, since both emphasized grace over acts, encouraging the cant which Parson Williams preaches, ''tis not what we do, but what we believe, that must save us' (*JA/S* 336).

By condensing *Pamela's* leisurely chapters into a few hectic lines, Fielding homes in on the moral ambiguities, which are linked, in his view, to the unconvincing characterization. The compression and accelerated pace show Richardson's vaunted psychological realism to be patently unreal, such as Mr B——'s shifts between abject love and frustrated anger.

> How can you say I would ruin you, answered the Squire, when you shall not ask anything which I will not grant you. If that be true, says I, good your Honour let me go Home to my poor but honest Parents; that is all I have to ask, and do not ruin a poor Maiden, who is resolved to carry her Vartue to the Grave with her.
>
> Hussy, says he, don't provoke me, don't provoke me, I say. You are absolutely in my power and if you won't let me lie with you by fair Means, I will by Force. O la, Sir, says I, I don't understand your paw Words. – Very pretty Treatment indeed, says he, to say I use paw Words; Hussy, Gipsie, Hypocrite, Saucebox, Boldface, get out of my Sight, or I will lend you such a Kick in the – I don't care to repeat the Word, but he meant my hinder part. (*JA/S* 339)

As Fielding sweeps together the scattered, angry epithets of Mr B—— into ludicrous lists, the welter of reported action and speech does not exactly resemble farce, but something even more absurd, someone describing a play at high speed – rendering *Pamela* itself as 'a farce'. But in a scene like this, something else is happening that takes Fielding's short work out of the realm of burlesque. His own blatant enjoyment of his performance is transferred to his central character and she acquires her own fictional authenticity. Her gutsy, breathless energy is endearing, and her delight in machinations is infectious:

31

I counterfeit a Swoon. Mrs. *Jervis* then cries out, O, Sir, what have you done, you have murthered poor *Pamela*: she is gone, she is gone. –

O what a Difficulty it is to keep one's Countenance, when a violent Laugh desires to burst forth. (*JA/S* 330)

As one peels off the onion layers that surround her story, the parodic Shamela ironically comes to seem the most honest character of all, since at least she acknowledges what she is doing. A further joke is the unstated fact that by the actual self-interested, mercantile standards of her day, Shamela is acting in the 'right' way and so deserves the marriage she finally wins. She is a good little capitalist, preferring contracts to promises, determined to protect her assets: 'nothing under a regular taking into Keeping, a settled Settlement, for me, and all my Heirs, all my whole Life-time, shall do the Business – or else cross-legged is the Word, faith, with *Sham*; and then I snapt my Fingers' (*JA/S* 330). But, like Defoe's Moll Flanders, another thoroughgoing, amoral, materialist 'innocent', Shamela has a fatal flaw, her weakness for a particular man. In a final postscript, Tickletext, cured of his Pamela fever, tells us tersely that Mr Booby 'hath caught his Wife in bed with *Williams*; hath turned her off, and is prosecuting him in the spiritual Court' (*JA/S* 357). This, too, is part of her appeal: having gained the heights, she loses all for love. Shamela, of course, has fallen for the biggest hypocrite of all, Parson Williams, the man who seduces through sermons. Her own technique is turned against herself.

Fielding is fond of Shamela: in some respects she is the innocent, the gull. The blame, he implies, lies less with her than with those who claim to 'guide' her, her mother and men like Williams. It is they (and writers like Richardson) who teach her the values she holds and the language which disguises them. Her blunt assertion, 'I once thought of making a little Fortune by my Person. I now intend to make a great one by my Vartue' (*JA/S* 342), *looks* like the core of the piece, but a harsher model is suggested by the constant repetition and play with the word 'Vartue' and by Shamela's silent thought, '*O what a charming word that is, rest his Soul who first invented it*' (*JA/S* 339).

Richardson's Pamela is a dangerous model, in Fielding's view, not because she is a maid skilfully angling for her master, but because she and the reader do not *see* that that is what she is, since the narrow physical meaning put on 'virtue' has been so thoroughly internalized. Pamela's very 'innocence' is her most pernicious attribute, and the danger is increased because the way the book is written – the letters, the immediacy, the detail, the seething urgency of tone – sucks the reader into the heroine's mentality.

Fielding thus suggests that the simulated morality is matched by a simulated realism. The whole edifice depends on the reader's collusion: the authenticity of the novel is essentially phoney since the familiar conventions of romance ensure the tale will end in marriage. We can indulge in Pamela's trials without real alarm – as voyeurs rather than sympathizers. Those who praise the book's morality are hypocritical as *readers*, wilfully blind to literary context, surrendering to the artifice of surface. By mimicking Richardson's technique, Fielding strikes at the 'truthfulness' of his method of representation. Parson Oliver does not only unmask the 'true name of this Wench', but unmasks the fraud of the epistolary form itself, offering his creator's wonderfully wild parodic version, 'in the following Letters, which I assure you are authentick' (*JA/S* 325). This insight into the moral coercion of form underlies Fielding's next move – the creation of a new moral genre of his own to tackle the problem of 'false-seeming'.

3

Form and Falsity: *Joseph Andrews*

Parody alone could not satisfy Fielding's irritation with Richardson. He wanted to show that there was another way of writing which would free 'virtue' from the purely sexual connotation, show that passions were not confined to desire, and place the ideals and actions of men and women in the wider context of the world. He would replace the static scenes, curtained rooms, walled gardens, locked houses – the boxes within boxes of Pamela's world – with the road and the inn, open to all, and give us mixed humanity instead of pure heroine and black villain. In the process he would uncover the flaws that he found in Richardson's work and in contemporary society – the mistaking of surface for depth, the gulf between outer and inner worth.

Shamela caused a stir in 1741 and was then ignored (swept under the carpet by Fielding's Victorian admirers as too crude, too bawdy), until it was reprinted in 1926. By contrast, *Joseph Andrews*, Fielding's second assault on *Pamela*, grew in reputation, acclaimed as the first English comic novel. 'The novel' in various forms, was far from new: Elizabethan prose fiction had been followed by translations of dense, fantastical multi-volume romances from France and Spain; Defoe had introduced a moral quasi-realism in the fictional biographies of *Robinson Crusoe* (1719) and *Moll Flanders* (1722), while the vogue for epistolary romance, exploited by Eliza Haywood and others, had been given a new, bourgeois twist by Richardson. Fielding knew, however, that he was springing something unexpected on the public with this 'comic-epic Poem in Prose'. He was moving from popular, visual, theatrical burlesque into a form addressed to a more literate, predominantly bourgeois public; a shift, as Judith Frank has shown, which affected the attitudes, as well as the aesthetics, of his writing.[1] Forestalling confusion, Fielding warns that readers accustomed to existing fictions may 'expect a kind of Entertainment, not to be found, nor which was even intended, in the following Pages' and introduces his book as 'a kind of Writing which I do not remember to have seen hitherto attempted in our language' (*JA/S* 53).

The reversal of expectations (of both readers and characters) is the novel's basic tactic, at once structural, critical, and moral. The starting-point is an inversion of *Pamela*. In place of Pamela under threat from Mr B——, we have her brother Joseph beleaguered by Lady Booby: it is not the heroine but the villainess who protests her 'virtue'. Instead of gaining a high marriage by his resistance, Joseph chooses a 'low' one to Fanny. Rather than good characters practising 'gentility', it is the 'bad' who affect it – Mrs Slipslop or Miss Grave-Airs. Instead of the ineffectual Mr Williams, we find the absent-minded Abraham Adams, with his cassock hanging below his greatcoat, his feet flying and his fists flailing.

The fast-flowing action is enriched by the interlocking allusions so characteristic of Fielding. The names of the main characters promise a moral tale (as *Pamela* purported to be), since the Old Testament Joseph and Abraham were standard sermon exempla for Chastity and Charity, private and general virtues, checking 'natural' greed and desire. This is indeed integral to the novel's meaning, but the ancestors Fielding claimed for his hybrid form are secular, not sacred: Homer's lost 'comic epic' the *Margites*, and Cervantes' *Don Quixote*. Fielding's blueprint is the *Odyssey*, with its 'series of actions all tending to produce one great end' (as he describes it in the Preface to *David Simple*, the novel by his sister Sarah Fielding).[2] The adventures of Joseph and Adams on the road home from London hark jokingly back to Odysseus traipsing home from Troy. But critics have pointed out that in Fénelon's *Aventures de Télémaque* (also mentioned by Fielding) the vengeful deity who blights Odysseus' path is Venus rather than Homer's Poseidon, a model hinted at by Joseph fleeing from Lady Booby. This lets Fielding mix Homeric burlesque (the dawn at Towwouse's inn, the description of Joseph's cudgel, the epic 'list' of hounds who pursue Parson Adams) with the heightened language of Romance, used sarcastically to deride Lady Booby and affectionately to dignify Fanny.

The stylistic patterning is itself part of a moral programme. The opening chapters to Books II and III, ('Of Divisions in Authors', 'Matter prefatory in Praise of *Biography*') deliberately draw attention to the artifice, and the ideological bias of representation. Fielding invokes his literary authorities seriously, but also renders the 'separate life' of a book with comic physicality – chapters are principally useful to prevent forgetful readers turning down pages. Fiction, he suggests, is a commodity, a matter for consumption and digestion, its production governed by an implicit contract between provider and consumer: 'it becomes an Author generally to divide a Book, as it doth a Butcher to joint his Meat, for such Assistance is of great Help to both the Reader and the Carver' (*JA/S* 80).

In *Joseph Andrews* Fielding manipulates conventions and styles like a musician transposing his theme into different modes, harmonies, and keys. The arithmetical proportions of the four books, totalling sixty-four chapters, with the square number (as in the last book's sixteen chapters) signifying harmony and justice, summon an old numerological convention, while the narrative deliberately sets the fluidity of the road and the whirl of chance against that controlling pattern. Like Adams, Fielding can balance on the brink of absurdity because his underlying conceptual structure is so solid. The action is skilfully kept *just* within the bounds of probability, and the most apparently spontaneous incidents turn out to be meticulously timed, like the overlapping journeys as Lady Booby and her entourage pursue Joseph. On close examination even the seemingly chaotic brawls are choreographed precisely.

The episodic narrative creates the kind of looseness Fielding had enjoyed in his plays, leaving room for many topical allusions. In passing he can praise his friends – Kitty Clive, Ralph Allen, William Hogarth – and mock his enemies, like Hervey, caricatured as Beau Didapper. Although he sometimes seems to patronize his lower-class protagonist, he can embrace low life as well as high, indulging his love of slang and of overblown pastiche, with the 'Ludicrous' in diction, as he calls it, replacing the epic sublime. The seemingly casual encounters allow him to insert stories, like those of Leonora and Mr Wilson, which expand the frame of reference beyond the immediate plot. More importantly, the form allows Fielding to create a nuanced rather than a schematic moral universe. Following Cervantes, he shows a comic, battling idealism confronting cynical realism and self-ishness in the expected upholders of charity and justice — the gentry, aristocracy, lawyers, and priests.

Fielding's stated aim is to expose the 'Ridiculous' – not pure good, or pure evil, which belong to Tragedy, but the middle area, the dangerous deceptions and self-deceptions arising from vanity and hypocrisy, the terrain of Comedy. The comic in this sense, derived from Molière and Ben Jonson, entertains and teaches through stylized imitation of nature, creating a realism of general truths through particular representation. Characters are immedi-ately placed by mannerisms: Slipslop with her garbled words, 'If we like a Man the lightest Hint *sophisticates*' (*JA/S* 28); Mrs Tow-wouse ready to send the injured Joseph packing; '"Common Charity a F—t!"' says she' (*JA/S* 50); the Doctor flourishing his latin tags; the false-lawyer Scout with his pedantic casuistry; the guzzling bully Parson Trulliber, with his 'I caal'd vurst' (*JA/S* 148). No one would ever really talk this way, but through such verbal shorthand Fielding can create a range of characters to whom readers react with amused recognition, not of an individual but of a type ('Oh, yes, I know someone exactly like that'). These vivid pictures were what Hazlitt most admired in Fielding, a sense of richly experienced life which subverted the pomp of official histories by suggesting 'the very web and texture of society as it really exists'.[3]

Behind his 'type' characters lies acute observation. Joseph and Fanny are recognizable juvenile leads, all feeling and ideals, but they are brought to life by realistic reactions, like Joseph's impatient response to Adams' counsel of Stoicism – 'easier to give Advice than take it' (*JA/S* 278) – after watching Adams weep with grief then dance with delight on thinking his son drowned and then finding him alive. Passing remarks show how fully imagined these characters are – like the comment in the middle of the bed-swapping at Booby Hall that Fanny is not disturbed when Adams slips in beside her because he turns the covers down so softly 'a Custom Mrs Adams had long accustomed him to' (*JA/S* 301). In this aside we glimpse years of late nights poring over Aeschlyus or writing sermons, oblivious of time.

In fiction Fielding could combine depth of detail with breadth of action. We still sense the debt to the theatre right up to the finale, when the story of Joseph and Fanny (having dipped towards disaster as it seems they may be brother and sister) is saved in a triumphant discovery scene, complete with exchanged infants and identifying birthmark. But the real difference is the extra dimension gained from authorial intervention, direct and indirect. In the early dialogues between Lady Booby and Slipslop, Lady Booby's fluctuating feelings towards Joseph are physically 'staged' by her constantly dismissing and recalling her maid. But at the same time she is implicitly criticized and rendered absurd by Fielding's commentary and stylistic games. The inflated classical allusions and invocations to Love – whose ability to overturn human reason is bathetically compared to the metamorphoses of Rich's Pantomimes and Cibber's distortion of grammar – convey both the falseness of her feelings and the way this falsity is typical of contemporary culture. There is a constant double perspective: the actions of the character filtered through the blatant manipulation of the author. Lady Booby is further ridiculed, for example, when Fielding echoes her language in his descriptions of Slipslop, who also fancies Joseph. Lust makes them equal, but Slipslop knows her own interests and is the more pragmatic:

> and being a little inclined to the Opinion of that Female Sect, who hold one lusty young Fellow to be near as good as another lusty young Fellow, she at last gave up *Joseph* and his Cause, and with a Triumph over her Passion highly commendable, walked off with her Present, and with great Tranquillity paid a visit to a Stone-Bottle, which is of sovereign Use to a Philosophical Temper. (*JA/S* 39)

Like Adams turning down the sheets, this off-stage scene is typical Fielding: an ironic blend of mock-solemn detachment and knowing sympathy. The grandiose terms applied to Slipslop's resort to booze also remind us to distrust style and watch for substance, which may *not* be the same as content. Thus much later, still rationalizing her desire for a footman, Lady Booby bewails the hypocrisy of high society:

> 'to shun the Contempt of others we must ally ourselves to those we despise: we must prefer Birth, Title and Fortune to real Merit. It is a Tyranny of Custom, a Tyranny we must comply with: For we People of Fashion are the Slaves of Custom.' (*JA/S* 265)

She speaks truth, but we (and Slipslop) know that her sentiments are not sincere but merely a useful face-saving strategy. The balanced sentences and disinterested content mask unbalanced emotion and cynical self-interest.

Similarly, while Adams and Joseph certainly retreat from the corrupt city to the 'pure' country, whose values they embody, Fielding is quick to suspect any pastoral–arcadian rhapsodies. Lady Booby herself sheds them abruptly when others talk of Fanny's rustic charms: 'Ridiculous! Beauty indeed, – a country Wench a Beauty. – I shall be sick whenever I hear Beauty mentioned again' (*JA/S* 252). People use and drop such language as it suits them, like Peter Pounce, who claims that the distresses of mankind are mostly imaginary, 'and it would be Folly to relieve them':

> 'Sure Sir,' replied Adams, 'Hunger and Thirst, Cold and Nakedness, and other Distresses which attend the Poor, can never be said to be imaginary Evils.' 'How can any Man complain of Hunger,' said Peter, 'in a Country where such excellent Sallads are to be gathered in almost every Field? or of Thirst, where every River and Stream produces such delicious Potations?' (*JA/S* 245)

Pounce has already been defined as 'an Hypocrite, a sort of People whom Mr Adams never saw through' (*JA/S* 240), but this is only one of many encounters where Adams is shocked by the degree to which he differs from someone with whom he believed he agreed. The key mood of *Joseph Andrews* is not suspense, but surprise: at different times all the characters, not only Adams, are 'confounded', 'astonished', 'struck dumb'. When Joseph is dismissed, we are told: 'As a Person who is struck through the Heart with a Thunderbolt, looks extremely surprised, nay, and perhaps is so too. Thus poor Joseph received the false Accusation of his Mistress' (*JA/S* 34). On the road, the tone is set by the 'Good Samaritan' episode, where the Postillion of a passing coach hears the groans of Joseph, who has been beaten by highwaymen. The coachman wants to leave him, for 'we are confounded late, and have no time for dead Men', but

> A Lady, who heard what the Postillion said, and likewise heard the Groan, called eagerly to the Coachman, 'to stop and see what was the matter.' Upon which he bid the Postillion 'alight, and look into the Ditch.' He did so, and returned, 'that there was a Man sitting upright as naked as ever he was born,'– 'O – *J-sus*,' cry'd the Lady, 'A naked Man! Dear Coachman, drive on and leave him.' (*JA/S* 46)

The agog curiosity and shocked prudery, the coy 'Jesus' and 'Dear Coachman', are deftly undercut by the Lady's fundamental callousness, but the overall impact of the scene, and its message about the rarity of charity, come from the subsequent piling-on of reactions. The other people on the coach – the two gentlemen and the lawyer – also give sound reasons for leaving Joseph, and then (having decided to take him in because they fear the legal consequences) steadfastly refuse him their coats. In the end the person who gives up his greatcoat is the least respectable, the Postillion, later to be transported for 'robbing a Hen-roost' (*JA/S* 47), just as, much later, the person who bails out Joseph and Adams when they cannot pay the bill is not a rich man but a travelling pedlar. (But, as Michael McKeon points out, these examples, which might seem to prove that degrees of virtue are in inverse ratio to class, could also be seen as simply establishing 'the basic paradox that if charity involves giving something for nothing, only those with nothing are likely to be charitable.'[4])

The technique of exposure through the characters' responses – like the switch in innkeepers' attitudes when they think Adams or Joseph do or do not have money or connections – is interwoven with action where events themselves bring surprises, reversals of expectation, and criticism of attitudes and institutions. Chains of episodes, brusquely interrupted just as they reach a climax, build into complex sequences. The ferociously patriotic Man of Courage flees on hearing a woman's screams, while the clergyman, Adams, stays and fights; the assaulted 'stranger' turns out to be Fanny; the 'helpers' Adams welcomes carry them off to the Justice; the intemperate Justice is about to send Adams to gaol when the Squire recognizes him; once established as a 'Gentleman' his conviction is immediately overturned.

The boldness of the action is matched by the daring tonal swings. In the encounters I have just mentioned, threatened rape, arrest, and imprisonment force the comedy perilously close to true misery: elsewhere, as at Booby Hall, seriousness risks being wiped out by farce. Even Lady Booby wants to laugh at Slipslop in bed with Adams (he has responded to Slipslop's screams when Beau Didapper leaps upon her, thinking she is Fanny, but grabs the wrong person). This could come straight from the stage, as could the scene when Adams mistakes his room:

> *Fanny* waking at the same instant, and stretching out her Hand on
> *Adams*'s beard, she cry'd out, – 'O Heavens! where am I?' 'Bless me!
> where am I?' said the Parson. Then *Fanny* skreamed, *Adams* leapt out
> of Bed, and Joseph stood, as the Tragedians call it, like the *Statue of
> Surprize*. 'How came she into my room?' cry'd Adams. 'How came you into
> hers?' cry'd Joseph in an Astonishment. (*JA/S* 302)

A prime joke is that the guileless Adams succeeds in getting into
Fanny's bed, where all the lustful men have failed. The style is
purely comic, but the chapter heading could stand for the
Parson's role in the whole novel' *'in which* Mr Adams *fell into many
Hair-breadth 'Scapes, partly owing to his Goodness, and partly to his
Inadvertency' (JA/S* 298). In these 'Night-Adventures' Adams is
literally exposed, in all his naked innocence.

In a curious way, Adams's very eccentricity makes him credible.
He was drawn partly from Fielding's absent-minded friend, the
Dorset curate Andrew Young, but he too is a literary type,
resembling his forebear Don Quixote in his idealism, his reliance
on ancient authorities, his stubborn judging of life from books.
One might suspect that Fielding (who is, after all, his creator) is
deliberately making Adams look ridiculous, as if his concept of
Charity is as archaic as Quixote's chivalry, unsuited to the modern
world of money and 'Law'. But whereas Quixote's courtly world
is sheer illusion, so that his adherence to it really *is* mad, Adams's
Classical–Christian ideals of honour, compassion, generosity, and
self-sacrifice *are* still, theoretically, those of his society. It is
because almost everyone he meets pays lip-service to the ideals he
lives by that he is so constantly disconcerted. Through him the
reader gradually begins to share the puzzlement that words and
acts, outer appearance and inner meaning, can so differ. Adams is
the ideal clergyman sketched in the *Champion*. He may be an
object of contempt for 'Boys and Beaus, and Madmen, and Rakes
and Fools', but beneath the odd appearance he is 'humble,
charitable, benevolent, void of Envy, void of Pride, void of Vanity,
void of Rapaciousness, gentle, candid, truly sorry for the Sins and
Misfortunes of men, and rejoicing in their Virtue and Happiness'
(C. 283).

In *Joseph Andrews* Fielding went much further than his original
intention of overturning the narrow morality of *Pamela*. True to his
Preface and to the programme of the *Champion*, he exposes the

vain and the hypocritical, the lustful and the mean. Some characters are clearly beyond redemption (the grasping Pounce, or the cruel, salacious Squire), but the dominant feeling is not negative but genial, lightened by the brio of the multi-layered comedy. The novel's warmth derives chiefly, however, from Fielding's determined optimism, which transcends his scepticism about the possibility of active virtue. Through the stories of Joseph and Adams he celebrates both enduring private love (in pointed contrast to the fashionable infatuations of Lady Booby) and the generalized love of mankind, true charity which must be critical as well as kind. Despite Fielding's witty disclaimers, the ending of his 'authentic History' of Pamela's brother Joseph still has its touch of Utopian romance.

4

Vice and Vision: *Jonathan Wild* and *A Journey from This World to the Next*

1

Joseph Andrews was published in February 1742, and, although friends of Richardson, like George Cheyne, declared it 'a wretched Performance' which 'will entertain none but Porters or Watermen', praise far outweighed criticism.[1]

That spring, however, Fielding could not rejoice. Three weeks after the novel appeared his 5-year-old daughter died in a raging flu epidemic. After a severe winter, his wife was also ill and he himself was beginning to suffer from gout. To augment his legal fees, he made brief forays back to play-writing in collaboration with David Garrick, and translated Plautus with Andrew Young. Neither scheme proved lucrative, but his proposal for a three-volume *Miscellanies* gained an impressive list of subscribers. Published in April 1743, Volume I included uncollected essays and poems such as the love lyrics to 'Celia' (Charlotte), and the verse essays 'Of True Greatness', 'Of Good-Nature' and 'On Liberty'. Volume II held *A Journey from This World to the Next* and two unpublished plays, while Volume III contained *Jonathan Wild*. (The form in which we usually read *Jonathan Wild* today, however, and the one quoted here, is the 1754 version, as revised by Fielding just before his death.)

Two of the essays in the *Miscellanies I* are of special interest. 'On Conversation' treats the typical Augustan theme of 'Man as a Social Animal', in which conversation, in the double sense of talk and acts, binds society together. As a guiding principle, Fielding chooses 'good-breeding', the practical expression of the rule *'Do unto all Men as you would they should do unto you'* (*M*. 124). Through a series of illustrations he carefully steers the notion of breeding away from class towards the following conclusion:

> That whoever, from the Goodness of his Disposition or Under-standing, endeavours to his utmost to cultivate the Good-humour and Happiness of others, and to contribute to the Ease and Comfort of all his Acquaintance, however low in Rank Fortune may have placed him, or however clumsy he may be in Figure or Demeanour, hath, in the truest Sense of the Word, a Claim to Good Breeding. (*M*. 152)

This conviction pervades Fielding's fiction. Sometimes, though, especially when the good character is indeed low in rank (like Joseph Andrews, Heartfree in *Jonathan Wild*, or Serjeant Atkinson in *Amelia*), the note of moral egalitarianism is sounded rather loudly and awkwardly – as if in reality he found it hard to dissociate true 'good-breeding' from aristocratic style.

If 'On Conversation' is the key to the non-heroic affability of heroes, then 'On the Knowledge of the Characters of Men' is a guide to Fielding's villains. In this sustained assault on hypocrisy (written more in the tradition of the homily than the discursive essay), Fielding describes character as a product of both nature and nurture. Thus an innate tendency to the bad, nourished by contemporary education (which teaches 'to conceal Vices rather than cultivate Virtues' (*M*. 154)) produces men who are masters of the *'Art of Thriving'*. Here Fielding tackles the idea of a deliberately cultivated acquisitive ambition, originally defined by Aristotle, which lies behind Machiavelli's notions of statecraft. The art of 'Thriving' is

> the very Reverse of that Doctrine of the Stoics; by which Men were taught to consider themselves as Fellow-Citizens of the World, and to labour jointly for the common Good, without any private Distinction of their own. Whereas *This*, on the contrary, points out to every Individual his own particular and separate Advantage, to which he is to sacrifice the Interest of all others; which he is to consider as his *Summum Bonum*, to pursue with his utmost Diligence and Industry, and to acquire by all Means whatever. (*M*. 154–5)

The essential 'means' is deceit: a victim has to be made to believe that 'he will be a Gainer by coming into those Schemes, which are, in Reality, calculated for his Destruction. And this, if I mistake it not, is the very Essence of that excellent Art, called *The Art of Politics'* (M. 155).

2

Jonathan Wild illustrates this 'Art of Politics'. The real Jonathan Wild was a contemporary legend, a man who rose from petty crook to master criminal through a genius for organization and intimidation. Never on the actual scene of a crime, he directed robberies and sold the goods back to their owners, claiming to have found them. In addition, he wiped out rivals and dissident members of his own gang by ruthlessly handing them over to arrest and execution, picking up rewards as a public-spirited 'thief-taker'. He was finally arrested after legal loopholes concerning the handling of stolen goods were closed, and his execution in 1725, as reported by Defoe, was marked by the degree of hatred shown by the triumphant crowd, rather than the usual sympathy.

In adapting Wild's story, Fielding characteristically fuses existing forms. First, he takes the commonplace satire of politicians as thieves (as in *The Beggar's Opera*), and in particular the analogy of Walpole and Wild. This connection had been suggested as early as 1725 in the anonymous *Life of Jonathan Wild, Thief-taker General*, whose mock-admiring style also presents Wild as an example of 'genius' and 'greatness'. Behind this kind of criminal biography lies the ballad and broadsheet formula of rogue as hero dating back to Elizabethan days. Fielding blends these popular traditions with a mock-heroic parody of the classical Plutarchian lives of great men. This broadens the political attack, in line with Enlightenment readings of history, to present all despots as criminal: in a 'great' conqueror or statesman, goodness is a weakness, to be criticized, not praised.

His master-stroke is to let Wild make the parallels himself. Wild is sure he is just as able as Alexander or Charles XII, but wiser and wilier, choosing to be a big fish in a small pond rather than dissipating his energies in a wider sphere. Throughout, 'Greatness', as a debased concept, is flagged in the same way that 'Vartue' is in *Shamela*. In the Preface to the *Miscellanies* as a whole, Fielding defensively separates 'the Great and Good' (the 'true

Sublime' in nature) both from non-heroic Goodness, a quality which arouses love rather than wonder (as shown in Heartfree), and from Greatness without goodness (as seen in Wild). This deformed Greatness is the false heroic, like the 'False Sublime' in poetry, whose bombast is often mistaken for true eloquence. The political parallels are pressed home by Wild's inveterate double dealings, his manipulative speeches, intimidation, pragmatism, opportunism, and talent for self-preservation. Ambition is combined with compulsive (and collusive) pretence: Wild and his first partner, the Count de la Ruse, never openly acknowledge they know the other is a crook, but double-cross each other whenever they can. The empty principles of political parties are mocked in the chapter 'On Hats'. The way all parties shed principles once they win power is suggested when Wild deposes Johnson, the Newgate 'king', on the grounds that he is 'usurping the liberties' of the prisoners, and then immediately becomes just as dictatorial.

In particular Fielding strikes at Wild's gift for getting his dirty work done by others, twisting their weaknesses and greed to ensure his continued dominance and to dispose of rivals:

> With such infinite Address did this truly great Man know how to play with the Passions of Men, to set them at variance with each other, and to work his own Purposes out of those Jealousies and Apprehensions which he was wonderfully ready at creating by means of those great Arts which the Vulgar call Treachery, Dissembling, Promising, Lying, Falsehood, etc., but which are by great Men summed up in the collective Name of Policy, or Politics, or rather *Pollitrics*; an Art of which, as it is the highest Excellence of Human Nature, perhaps our great Man was the most eminent Master. (*JW* 102)

As Fielding says in the Preface, while no one should mistake Newgate for 'Human Nature with the Mask on', one might well be excused 'for suspecting that the Palaces of the Great are often no other than *Newgate* with the Mask on' (*JW* 10). But, as often in Fielding, the satire is not so clear as it seems: the critique of courts and Palaces of the Great is, after all, offset by the principal story – a burlesque of the aspiring, upwardly mobile, self-made man.

The satire is further complicated by the story of the Heartfrees, Wild's main victims. This emphasizes the personal rather than the political depths and dangers of 'The Art of Thriving', dramatizing both Wild's confident treachery and his paranoid insecurity. It also lets Fielding introduce other forms to extend the argument. There are echoes of Bunyan in Heartfree's trials and language, particularly his prison soliloquy. Mrs Heartfree's adventures abroad allow a conventional view of the relative honour of 'savage' societies. But the parody of current travel-writings (in the first version she even tramps through the body of an elephant) makes her credibility as dubious as Wild's. Once freed of her family, she seems startlingly independent, even rogue-like, returning with her jewels like a successful profiteer. Similarly, her sexual vulnerability adds comedy, with moments of supreme illogic like the Captain's furious question to Wild, 'if he had no more Christianity than to ravish a Woman in a Storm?' (*JW* 114). But the near-rapes (and the way Mrs Heartfree uses them to inspire protection) also highlight the way 'great' men see the world as food for their insatiable appetites. Critics who prefer unified literary forms object to Heartfree as sentimental and Mrs Heartfree as digressive. But the 'silly' innocence and domesticity of the man, the courage and endearing vanity of the woman, metaphorically fling open the gates of the prison within which the political satire on its own would confine us.

The formal and conceptual mixture is grotesque and real, sentimental and stern. Whereas in *Joseph Andrews* Fielding claimed to draw from Nature, comparing his art to Hogarth's comic paintings, here he uses blackly comic caricature, like Hogarth's deliberately simplified engravings for his didactic series of prints *Industry and Idleness* and *The Four Stages of Cruelty*. The harsh outlines are needed, because the subject is not just false morality but outright evil, the murderous connivings of a master criminal or political tyrant. Fielding enforces detachment. His purpose is to wake readers up to the tricks that are being played on them – by the author as well as by the subject of his fiction. To show how we build myths in defiance of fact, he openly falsifies Wild's biography, giving him a mock genealogy of sticky-fingered forebears, placing his birth during the Fire of London, attended by comical dreams and portents, and providing the requisite marvels of youthful prowess and classical examples. He is intent on showing his hand. Stylistically, this is Fielding's most lawyer-like book: Wild's speeches are repeatedly constructed in terms of axiom, deduction, and evidence. So it comes as a shock when he writes his wondrously illiterate letter to Laetitia, 'It would be the hiest Preassumption to imagin you eggnorant of my Loav' (*JW* 140). At this point Fielding 'confesses' that this may look odd after the eloquent speeches that he, the author, has given him. In other words, readers have been as stupid to 'believe' in these speeches as Wild's hearers within the fiction.

Jonathan Wild recalls Fielding's attack on *Pamela*: being dupéd by the style – of a person, a speech, or a book – leads 'ordinary people' to collude in the wrongs of the world. The fault lies deeper than credulity, amounting almost to a positive desire to be taken in, because it is easier than thinking for ourselves. The book is full of examples of the way people persuade themselves that appearances are true. When Heartfree is accused of embezzlement, Fielding notes a curious fact, 'though we doubt it will appear very unnatural and incredible to our Reader; which is, that, notwithstanding the former Behaviour and Character of Heartfree, this Story of his Embezzling was so far from surprising his Neighbours, that many of them declared they expected no better from him' (*JW* 157). The point being that such switches in attitudes are all too natural and credible, and also that people are always ready to condemn others, given the chance.

To demonstrate this wil(d)ful gullibility (as well as the way Wild manipulates his gang), Fielding describes a puppet-show where the master of the show 'dances and moves everything'. Everyone knows he is there, but, because he does not appear, the audience obediently follow his whim, 'by calling the several Sticks or Puppets by the Names which the Master hath allotted to them, and by assigning to each the Character which the great Man is pleased they may move in' (*JW* 154). In a novel, the invisible author is the prime mover: in politics or crime we see the 'Great Man' but choose to remain blind to his dealings – until he falls from power. Overtly, this is a satire about illusory greatness: covertly, it is about persuasion and self-persuasion, and the role of self-interest in both. Both its humour and its note of threatening anarchy come from a meditation on human nature as a whole, not just the crimes of Wild or Walpole.

But Fielding, like Wild, is an inveterate double-dealer. While exposing Wild's horrifying ruthlessness, he constantly undercuts his hero's mock 'Greatness'. He is conned by the Count, stabbed by Blueskin Blake, cuckolded by his lieutenant Fireblood, robbed by Molly Straddle, and exploited and deceived by 'the chaste

Laetitia'. Sexually, he is so driven by his own desires that he cannot even see straight, finding Laetitia in 'the most beautiful Undress' (JW 63) when she is actually described with almost Swiftian disgust. Tactically, because he thinks everyone is like himself, he is a master of misjudgement, suggesting robbery and murder to the principled Heartfree.

Wild is blinded not only by greed, but by his own conviction of Greatness. His delusion that he is chosen by 'Destiny' or 'Nature' is always made ridiculous, especially when he decides to commit a glorious classical suicide after being marooned with no oars, no sail, and only biscuits between him and starvation. Having 'cast himself headlong into the sea', we next learn that he is 'miraculously within two minutes replaced in his Boat' (JW 119). But this is no ignominious scrabble back to safety. Nature, 'having originally intended our great Man for that final exaltation' we wish for all 'great' men (his hanging), refuses to be diverted.

> She, therefore, no sooner spied him in the Water than she softly whispered in his Ear to attempt the recovery of his Boat, which call he immediately obeyed, and, being a good Swimmer, and it being a perfect Calm, with great Facility accomplished it. (JW 119)

Fielding's undisguised delight in his mock form is felt in his dead-pan suggestion that he has been almost as heroic as Nature saving Wild, in rescuing his relation 'from the Prodigious, which though it often occurs in Biography, is not to be encouraged' (JW 119).

Although Brecht may, as has been suggested, have drawn on Wild for his study of tyranny in *Arturo Ui*,[2] ultimately Fielding is incapable of stern Brechtian detachment. Despite his moral outrage, the comic medium begins to dominate the message. Like Tom Thumb's, Wild's greatness is laughable because he is so 'small': the Newgate crown he takes from Johnson is too big for him, the shabby robes do not even keep him warm. Slowly his numbskull persistence almost wins sympathy. At the end, as he jokes about death, dozes through the discourse on Hell Fire, and swings out of the world with the Chaplain's (stolen) bottle-opener in his hand, the rogue begins to seem a hero after all. Part of the unease of this powerful little book comes from the author's own seduction by style, by the bombast of a figure who represents the very values Fielding most detests.

3

A Journey from This World to the Next is also a hybrid form, but one based on a genre which appeals less to modern readers. This is a pity, since it is intriguing and illuminating, containing some delightful writing and acting almost as a notebook of Fielding's leading concerns.

The use of a visit to the dead to comment on the ways of the living derives from 'the incomparable Lucian', the second-century Greek satirist and fantasist. The Lucianic journey had been used by Rabelais, Pope, and Swift, and once again Fielding both follows his forebears and turns the form to his own ends. He borrows the Scriblerian apparatus, as used in *The Tale of a Tub* or *The Dunciad*, presenting the book as a partial manuscript unearthed in a bookseller's shop, the rest 'being destroyed in rolling up Pens, Tobacco, &c' (*J*. 144). These convenient 'gaps' let him combine material written at different times (probably during 1741–2), and end as abruptly as he pleases. He also borrows the standard incompetent editor, who fusses about detail, misses the main point, and hints that the 'author' is a Bedlam madman. Since the editor himself is clearly an idiot, this invites readers to accept the 'mad' manuscript as sane, agreeing with the opinion of 'Parson Abraham Adams ... that there was more in it than first appeared' (*J*. 3).

The introduction of Adams is apt, not only because it reminds us to reverse superficial judgements, but because the *Journey* is a spiritual picaresque, complementing the secular adventures of *Joseph Andrews*. Instead of the road from London to Dorset, we travel through a metaphysical landscape which is fundamentally Platonic, with overtones of Bunyan and Swift. At the gates of Elysium, the dead are judged by the gatekeeper Minos. If found good, their souls may enter, after drinking the waters of oblivion to purge them of earthly passions. If inadequate, they return to earth, drawing lots from the Wheel of Fortune for a new incarnation. The jumbled manuscript falls into three sections. The first describes the narrator's journey and arrival, while the second recounts the many transmigrations of Julian the Apostate (the controversial and enigmatic fourth-century Roman Emperor who largely tolerated Christianity while rejecting the faith himself in favour of Greek religion and philosophy). The final part contains a rather limp and sentimental retelling of the life of Anne Boleyn. This is generally thought to have been written by Sarah Fielding, though Henry's tart tones are audible at the end, when Anne is allowed into Elysium:

> on the Consideration that whoever had suffered being the Queen for four years, and had been sensible during all that Time of the real Misery which attends that exalted Station, ought to be forgiven what she had done to attain it. (J. 144)

The first part contains some of Fielding's most engaging writing. Oddly, it is in the fantasy that one feels his 'realist' impulse most strongly. Each stage is visualized and made concrete through comic detail: the narrator's bothered soul, unable to escape the body because the mouth-door is shut and the eyes/windows closed, eventually escapes 'down through a kind of Chimney, and issued out of the Nostrils' (J. 5). His friends have left the death-bed and are quarrelling downstairs, and only an old woman remains, fast asleep after 'a comfortable Dose of Gin'. He jumps out of the window, discovering to his astonishment that he cannot fly ('owing probably, to my having neither Feathers nor Wings' (J. 5)) and is hopping cheerfully through the street when a tall young gentleman with silk waistcoat, garland, and caduceus introduces himself as Mercury: ' "Sure, Sir," said I, "I have seen you at the Playhouse" ' (J. 6). The game continues, as the spirits meet in the coach, all complaining of the cold and of 'how dark it was' (J. 8).

In a comic blurring of physical and spiritual, the narrator is smitten by a beautiful young female spirit who arouses 'a very violent Degree of seraphic Love' (J. 10). But satire has already entered fantasy – all passengers declare great satisfaction about their exit from a wicked world, yet all would have avoided the accident which caused it. The 'grave Lady' has left a doctor by her bedside; the gentleman who died of honour (in a duel) 'very liberally cursed both his Folly and his Fencing' (J. 11). From this it is easy for Fielding to slide into didacticism – the miser whose punishment is to hand out his gold to passing travellers; the City of Diseases; the Palace of Death, frequented by the great slayers, those heroes of Jonathan Wild: Louis XIV, Charles XII, Alexander. (But not the Duke of Marlborough, whose memory Fielding respected. Death has been badly served by this great British general who 'never sent him a single Subject he could keep from him, nor did he ever get a single Subject by his Means but he lost 1000 others for him' (J. 22)).

As we approach Elysium and see souls unfit for Paradise being given 'characters' to return to earth, the nutshell-stories achieve the compactness of moral or political diagrams. A defiant king, for example, sets off down the path of goodness: 'he was gone a little Way when a Spirit limped after him, swearing he would fetch him back. This Spirit, I was presently informed, was one who had drawn the Lot of his Prime Minister' (J. 28). Before drawing lots each spirit drinks different proportions of the 'pathetic Potion', which gives emotion, and the 'Nousphiric potion', granting brains (pretty women dislike the taste). The theory of humours merges with the belief in innate characteristics. A person is not a *tabula rasa*, a blank page, at birth.

Character, however, is also defined by circumstance and role. This is the linking theme of the stories of Julian the Apostate, who has been 'forced to undergo several subsequent Pilgrimages on Earth', in the shape of different characters ranging from 'a Slave, a Jew, a General', to 'a Poet, a Knight, a Dancing-Master and three times a Bishop' (J. 44). Only his final martyrdom in the form of 'the very individual Archbishop Latimer' gains him entrance to Elysium. Through Julian's many lives, Fielding shows the impact of education, expectation, and habit: tendencies are ordained, but finished character and destiny are contingent. He also argues that codes of behaviour, especially sexual morality, vary according to period and custom. This includes homosexuality, when placed in the context of classical hedonism:

> Perhaps you may admire at the close Union between this Priest and his Slave, but we lived in an Intimacy which the Christians thought criminal; but my Master, who knew the will of the Gods, with whom he often conversed, assured me it was perfectly innocent. (J. 48)

Despite this plea for moral pluralism, the sketches insist that heaven or hell is found on earth. The cruel, the vain, the ambitious are dogged by inner torments. The miser lives in dread, while the extravagant beau is rendered empty by surfeit because everything comes too quickly:

> I scarce ever knew the Delight of satisfying a craving Appetite. Besides, as I never once thought, my Mind was useless to me, and I

was an absolute Stranger to all the Pleasures arising from it ... in the midst of Plenty I loathed everything. (*J.* 59)

In contrast, the *Journey* has versions of happiness: the pastoral simplicities of Anne Boleyn tending her garden; the domestic life, gently mocked in Julian as a beggar, marrying for love, with nineteen children and a wife who still manages to get supper on time, 'this being my favourite Meal, and at which I, as well as my whole Family, greatly enjoyed ourselves' (*J.* 94). But Fielding's true Elysium is the realm of the imagination, a merry place, with concerts, picnics, and literary tomfoolery, where heroes meet their authors and, in an affectionate vignette, our narrator is warmly embraced by Tom Thumb.

Freed from the constraints of the real, Fielding assuages his grief, meeting his little daughter again and walking hand in hand through gentle fields. Yet his purpose is stern as well as consolatory. In the *Journey* the element of judgement which sustains his writing is brought firmly to the centre, but the judgements of Minos are often opposite to those the world might expect. They dissect motive as well as act, substituting a justice of feeling for that of law or religion. A man who has 'never once been guilty of Whoring, Drinking, Gluttony, or any other Excess' proudly declares he has disinherited his son for getting a bastard: '"Have you so" said Minos; "then pray return into the other world and beget another; for such an unnatural Rascal shall never pass this Gate"' (*J.* 31). The prude, the politician, the false patriot are turned back: the man hanged for robbery of eighteenpence who has been a tender son and father is admitted. So is the poet who gave the proceeds of his benefit to a friend 'and thus saved him from Destruction'. And so is our narrator:

> I confessed I had indulged myself very freely with Wine and Women in my youth, but had never done any Injury to any Man living, nor avoided an Opportunity of doing Good. That I pretended to very little Virtue more than general Philanthropy and private Friendship. I was proceeding when Minos bid me enter the Gate, and not indulge myself with trumpeting forth my Virtues. (*J.* 36)

This indulgent, self-mocking absolution is also a blueprint for Fielding's next hero – Tom Jones.

5

War, Women, and Worldly Judgement: *Tom Jones*

1

In late 1743, with the success of the *Miscellanies*, Fielding's situation looked relatively settled. He still travelled the Western Circuit, he had generous patrons, and he also had a new son, Harry. But over the winter all this good fortune was undermined by Charlotte's worsening health. One distraction was provided by Sarah Fielding, whose novel *David Simple* appeared in May 1744. In a Preface to the second edition, Henry suggested that the form the 'Moral Tale', the wanderings of an innocent youth in the city, may have drawn on his *Joseph Andrews*: in his view the novel's only faults lay in the want of 'learning'. Both points, understandably, may have piqued his sister: in *Familiar Letters of David Simple* (1747) she deliberately chose the epistolary style of Henry's rival Richardson, now her close friend, and she began studying Classics with zeal.

Fielding himself contributed five letters to *Familiar Letters*, including Valentine's praise of true, chaste, romantic married love. By then the theme was poignant, for his beloved Charlotte had died in Bath, in the winter of 1744. Lady Louisa Stuart, granddaughter of Lady Mary Wortley Montagu, later suggested that Henry's grief was compounded with guilt:

> Sometimes they were living in decent lodgings with tolerable comfort; sometimes in a wretched garret without necessaries; not to speak of the spunging houses and hiding places where he was occasionally to be found. His elastic gaiety of spirit carried him through it all; but meanwhile, care and anxiety were preying upon her more delicate mind, and undermining her constitution. She gradually declined,

caught a fever, and died in his arms.[1]

Contemporary stories show Fielding as either prostrated or wildly vivacious. These are not necessarily contradictory. He fought to find philosophic calm, asking himself, as he said he always did in a crisis, 'What would Socrates have done?', but his work is full of odd mood swings. Only in *Tom Jones*, written in bursts from 1745 to 1748, did he fully recover his 'elastic gaiety of spirits' and resurrect his lost Charlotte as Sophia, independent, spirited, and brimming with health.

After a year Fielding was galvanized into writing again by the Jacobite Rebellion. Charles Stuart, the Young Pretender, landed in the Hebrides in July 1745 and marched south as far as Derby before turning back; after his army had been annihilated at Culloden in April 1746, he fled back to France, leaving his followers to face mass executions and transportation. During the crisis Fielding ran a weekly journal, the *True Patriot*, containing stout Hanoverian leaders, comment on the progress of the Rising, and lively miscellaneous items. (Two years later his next paper, the *Jacobite's Journal*, lampooned the opposition through the blustering 'John Trott-Plaid'.) He saw the rising as a real and immediate threat. The *True Patriot* relates a vivid dream in which he is snatched from his study by armed Highlanders, who drag him to Newgate through corpse-littered streets. Tried before a Stuart court speaking mangled English, he is hauled off to execution, past many Protestant martyrs. Just as the noose tightens, he wakes. The spectres of intolerance, violence, and travesties of justice that stalk this dream would lurk in the background to *Tom Jones*.

Tom Jones is also concerned with internal threats to peace of mind, the urges of appetites and passions. This personal brand of danger is the theme of Fielding's strange, unsigned pamphlet, *The Female Husband*, also published in 1746. It deals with a scandal from his native town of Glastonbury, where a certain Mary Hamilton, posing as a doctor, had married a young woman. Fielding's cousin Henry Gould was a counsel for the prosecution, but, despite the title-page claim, 'Taken from her own mouth since her confinement', the pamphlet is largely fantasy. It begins with pot-boiling phrasing – 'abominable and unnatural pollutions', 'wicked crime', 'vile amours' (*FH* 30, 31) – using the time-honoured slur of linking non-conformism to unbridled sexuality (as in *Shamela*). But it is hard to judge Fielding's precise attitude: once he begins to write, his curiosity and sense of humour start to get the better of his moral outrage; and as he begins to enjoy the comic mechanics of deception and bodice-ripping disclosures, the story becomes extremely funny. Like Shamela, Mary is almost admirable in her brazen opportunism. Her youthful seduction is presented as a 'natural' extension of a passionate friendship: her real crime is not her sexual deviance but her hardened, opportunistic bigamy, which preys on ignorant dupes.

Yet it was that youthful 'natural' fall from grace which initially disturbed Fielding and led him to take up his pen. His opening strikes a note heard before in the *Champion*. When governed by 'virtue and religion', heterosexual desire produces 'the most rational felicity':

> but if once our carnal appetites are let loose, without those prudent and secure guides, there is no excess and disorder which they are liable to commit, even while they pursue their natural satisfaction; and, which may seem still more strange, there is nothing monstrous and unnatural, which they are not capable of inventing, nothing so brutal and shocking which they have not actually committed. (*FH* 29)

The Female Husband is an attack on the attitudes of mind which justify discarding those 'prudent and secure guides'.

In a prose paraphrase of Ovid's *Ars amatoria* (also 1746), at the end of a list of rape, incest, and bestiality, Fielding comments: 'All these have been the Effects of Womens raging Desires, which are so much more violent and mad than ours.'[2] It is tempting, but wrong, to identify him with Ovid's sentiment. In his fiction both sexes love (and brawl) with equal vigour. He certainly credits women with strong desires – from the animal high spirits of Molly Seagrim or the generous hedonism of Mrs Waters to predators like Shamela, Lady Booby or Lady Bellaston – but his amorous women are easily outnumbered by lustful, callous men, while his heroines (unlike most of his heroes) embody a sensuality controlled by nature and principle. He knew that men were as much victim of their own appetites as of women's.

In the mid-1740s Fielding was living with his sister Sarah, her friend Margaret Collier, and a 26-year-old housekeeper, Mary Daniel. Mary had comforted Henry after the death of Charlotte, and by the spring of 1747 she had become his mistress. That autumn, when she was six months pregnant, he married her. His enemies crowed with delight, but Fielding (possibly pressured by Lyttleton) saw the social 'disgrace' as a badge of honour, not dishonour like the marriage which Tom Jones urges on Nightingale: 'Can you with Honour, be the knowing, the wilful Occasion, nay, the artful Contriver of the ruin of a Human Being... Can you with Honour bear the Thought that this Creature is a tender, helpless, defenceless young Woman?' (*TJ* 678).

While never portraying female sensibility with the insight of Richardson, Fielding has immense sympathy for the legal and physical powerlessness of women: as daughters and wives, and as victims of sexual exploitation and social hypocrisy. The one character he allows a happy future, at the end of *Jonathan Wild*, is Theodosia Snap. Her pregnancy by the Count de la Ruse (whom she genuinely loves) had provoked an outburst from Laetitia at the family disgrace, prompting Theodora's expulsion from home and imprisonment in Bridewell, but finally, says Fielding, she was transported to America, where 'she was pretty well married, reformed, and made a good Wife' (*JW* 220).

Fielding's views on women shift according to context and mood: it is equally limited to interpret him as forwarding the feminist programme of Mary Astell[3] as it is to regard him (as Dr Johnson did) as recommending sexual immorality, or as adopting the cynicism of Pope's 'Characters of Women'. Sometimes he proclaims conventional assumptions: the ideal woman is beautiful, submissive, gentle, a mistress of the domestic arts, who can be ruined by scholarship as much as by frivolity. On the other hand, in journalism and fiction, he vehemently upholds women's property rights, laments their lack of legal status and inadequate education, attacks cruelty in marriage, and exposes the double sexual standard. In life, he supported his sister's writing and was always fond of unconventional women: the flamboyant, transvestite Charlotte Charke, the brilliant Kitty Clive, the bold, spirited Mary Wortley Montagu.

In the elaborate games of *Tom Jones*, women are both ladders and snakes, Tom's downfall and inspiration. As the object of Tom's love and the ultimate judge of his actions, Sophia (whose name means Wisdom) has a penumbra of symbolic power. Yet the rapturous, highly allusive introduction to her first appearance (often quoted as indicating her emblematic status) is deliberately undercut by the passing mention of 'the rude Answer Lord *Rochester* once gave a Man, who had seen many Things' (*TJ* 154). In other words, 'If you have seen all these, then kiss my arse.' As so often, Fielding warns against rhetoric and pedestals. Sophia was a picture of the woman he loved, and, as the subsequent blunt description so tenderly insists, she is not ideal but *real* – 'a middle-sized woman; but rather inclining to tall' (*TJ* 155). She is subject as well as object: her struggle for autonomy is of equal importance to Tom's story.

2

Tom Jones constantly sets illusion against reality in this way, keeping its readers as alert as a jury to issues of truth and misrepresentation, questioning 'evidence' in the light of intent, motive, and malice, showing how 'witnesses' are suborned by bribes, threats, and promises. Throughout, the interwoven narratives offer three touchstones for judgement: attitudes to women, to the poor, and to the nation. All are related to a subtle argument about principles of government and self-government.

The decision to set the novel against the background of the Rising was almost certainly taken after the first chapters were written. From then on, the atmosphere of threat and wild rumour, the ill-disciplined soldiers, and the blustering of Squire Western against the 'Hanoverian rats' lend a subterranean unease to the soaring comedy. We feel the strange way a war is experienced, its far-off rumblings at once insistent yet far less pressing than domestic rows, lost love, unpaid bills. Although Tom thinks it glorious to die for his country, most people have more immediate interests. The landlord who mistakes Sophia for Jenny Cameron, believing the rebels are *en route* for London, wants to curry favour with the victors. In a later inn-kitchen discussion, issues of hereditary right and religion quickly give way to self-interest: the landlady declares that Papists 'spend their Money very freely and it is always a Maxim with me that one Man's Money is as good as another's' (*TJ* 575); the puppet-show man doesn't care what religion comes, unless it be Presbyterians, 'for they are enemies to Puppet-shows' (*TJ* 575); the excise-man sticks with the government, despite his dislike of Popery, because he's bound to lose his place once his current patrons lose power. In the words of the puppet-master, 'To be sure, every man values his livelihood first, that must be granted' (*TJ* 575).

Partridge's Jacobitism is at one with his superstition, a regressive clinging to the old ways, a refusal to see things clearly. Squire Western, a hater of court and 'lords', clings to the Jacobite traditions of the squirearchy, despite his shrewd grasp of the new mercantile finances, the 'Politico-Peripatetic School of Exchange-Alley' (*TJ* 258). His 'progressive' sister is a stout Hanoverian, identifying with the court, the Whigs, and the fashions of the Town. As a motif in their long-running sibling battle, national politics are reduced to ludicrous childishness: ' "Ho! are you come back to your Politics," cries the Squire, "as for those I despise them as much as I do a F—t." Which last Word he graced with the very Action, which, of all others, was most proper to it' (*TJ* 308). However, absurd, the Westerns' prejudices reveal their misconceptions of 'good government', as important in a family as a nation. Western loves Sophia like an absolute monarch does his subjects, only as long as they carry out his wishes and aid his territorial ambitions. Her aunt's apparently liberal outlook is designed to make Sophia adept in the devious tactics of 'the world', whose goal is wealth and status. Both are equally blind to her feelings and true interests.

The theme of parents, children, and upbringing is stressed in the early chapters, as Thwackum, Square, and Allworthy apply their different principles (and interests) to the education of Tom and Blifil. But the argument – and its relation to wider issues of government, justice, and mercy – is sustained throughout the book by the portrayal of different parents, like the Nightingale brothers or Mrs Miller, and reflected in discussions of social organization like the benign despotism of the King of the Gypsies. Among the parents, only Mrs Miller wins whole-hearted approval:

> For as this good Woman had all the Tenderness, so she had preserved all the Authority of a Parent; and as her Indulgence to the Desires of her Children was only restrained by her Fears for their Safety and future Welfare, so she never suffered those Commands, which proceeded from such Fears, to be either disobeyed or disputed. (*TJ* 628)

But even she cannot assume control of other lives, as Nancy's pregnancy shows.

Nancy and Sophia are especially vulnerable simply because they are women. In Sophia's case, Fielding asserts the unconditional right of resistance against tyranny (Western) and greedy exploitation (Blifil); in Nancy's he argues that the strong (Nightingale) have a greater duty to the weak whom they exploit than to their own advancement. Both instances suggest political analogies, but Fielding (despite his fun at the expense of female scholarship, vanity, or shrewishness) is also clearly concerned with the particular issue, the plight of contemporary women. Almost every chapter contains an allusion to the powerlessness of women and the evils this induces. Bridget Allworthy obeys her brother outwardly but takes her own course, while she makes 'a few Observations, as that men were headstrong and must have their own Way, and would wish she had been blest with an independent Fortune' (*TJ* 60). Her marriage to the fortune-hunting Captain Blifil is one of mutual torment: she rejoices in his death and hates their son. Mrs Fitzpatrick, also entrapped for her money, escapes from a loveless imprisonment into the arms of a rich protector. Squire Western (like Parson Trulliber) treats his wife as a 'faithful upper Servant' (*TJ* 309), abusing her for 'Ingratitude' even after her death.

The legal assumption that women and their property are entirely at the disposal of fathers or husbands is matched by the sexual assumption that women on their own are fair game. The avid huntsman Western sees nothing inconsistent in hounding Black George for poaching, and applauding Tom for seducing Molly, Black George's daughter. 'Decent' women, too, like Deborah Wilkins or Mrs Honour, take the view that, 'when Wenches are so coming, young Men are not so much to be blamed neither; for to be sure they do no more than is natural' (*TJ* 188). Fielding did see sexual lapses as venial, not mortal, sins, but the reason we are asked to judge Tom lightly is that he is never the seducer. He simply responds – enthusiastically enough – to Molly's advances, after which his attitude (unlike Nightingale's to Nancy) is generous, compassionate, and responsible. The outcome of the sexy feast at Upton is manœuvred by Mrs Waters, after Tom has manfully resisted her bare-bosomed appeal on the road. In London he surrenders reluctantly to Lady Bellaston (significantly, at a masquerade) on grounds of gallantry and gratitude. His sexual escapades are thus an interesting conjunction of 'natural' moral instinct, an unselfish response to the wants of others, which is to be praised, and selfish 'natural' desires. The latter, as *The Female Husband* stressed, can lead to disaster if uncontrolled. Allworthy's lecture on chastity at the start of the book is balanced by the gulf of sexual horror that opens before Tom at the end. The prospect of his incest with Mrs Waters is not merely a last-minute cliff-hanger, but a vision of the unnatural acts to which natural appetite can unwittingly lead. Yet, even if it were true, one feels the absolution of comedy would have carried Tom through.

To begin with, in his feelings for Molly, Tom mistakes appetite for love. In the next stage, although he can now distinguish between the two, he is still comically capable of sinking into the bushes with Molly after sighing Sophia's name: only later does he feel that sex is empty without love. In the chapter 'On Love' Fielding traces this gradation from hunger, or lust, to the rapturous enjoyment when desire is joined to personal feeling. But he then extends his theme by linking the capacity for mutual love to that for a wider love for mankind. In this light, Tom's sexual responsiveness parallels his response to the poor, shown by gestures like his impulsive generosity to the highwayman. As in his dealings with women, self-interest and openness to the needs of others merge. He finds real pleasure in charity, even to the 'undeserving': his reward is not applause for righteousness but an almost sensual expansion of spirit. The sexual parallel is felt in Tom's own language (admittedly over a bottle of wine), when he tells Dowling he does not envy Blifil. What are worldly goods, he says, 'compared to the warm, solid Content, the swelling Satisfaction, the thrilling Transports, which a good Mind enjoys in the Contemplation of a generous, virtuous, noble, benevolent Action' (*TJ* 583).

Tom learns active benevolence from Allworthy, but it is also an expression of his own personality and principles. The latter, in his view, as he says of the rescue of Mrs Waters, simply embody the common duties of humanity. And when he faces an unpleasant decision, or is troubled as to correct actions, he tests it against an instinctive sense of 'honour'. 'Honour' decrees he offer to marry Molly, and places him in thrall to Lady Bellaston:

He had never less inclination to an Amour than at present, but Gallantry to the Ladies was among his principles of Honour, and he held it as much incumbent upon him to accept a Challenge to love, as if it had been a Challenge to fight. (*TJ* 633)

In the first instance, Fielding suggests Tom is right, in the second case he is wrong. 'Honour' is one of the most slippery terms in the book. (It is typical of the novel's rich texture that Sophia's maid, one of the most mendacious, garrulous, and loyalty-shifting characters, should be named Honour.) The first real trial of Tom's character is the childhood incident where he refuses to admit that Black George accompanied him when trespassing on Western's land. When betrayed by Blifil, he can only say that 'He scorned a Lie as much as Anyone, but he thought his Honour engaged him to act as he did; for he had promised the poor Fellow to conceal him' (*TJ* 132). Allworthy warms to him, but has already said he acted on 'a mistaken Point of Honour' (*TJ* 127). In the heated debate between Thwackum and Square on the question 'Can any Honour exist independent of Religion?', which merely shows that they define the term to support their opposing allegiances to religion or to 'the eternal Fitness of Things', Allworthy pointedly disagrees with both, saying he had said 'nothing of true Honour' (*TJ* 129).

What then is 'true honour'? The term intrigues Fielding, in that its meaning – unlike 'virtue' or 'charity' – shifts so sharply according to the goals of the individual or the mores of a particular milieu. In some senses honour (and the enforced duplicity and solidarity of women) provokes his plot, for Bridget Allworthy conceals Tom's birth to defend her 'honour', and Jenny Jones then lies because of her promise to Bridget, refusing 'to sacrifice either my Honour, or my Religion' (*TJ* 69). But, when Miss Western tells Sophia she ought to have a greater regard to the honour of her family than for her own person, she does not mean personal commitment to other family members but merely to name and property:

'Have you no sense of Ambition? Are there no Charms in the Thoughts of having a Coronet on your Coach?' 'None, upon my Honour,' said Sophia. 'A Pincushion upon my Coach would please me just as well.' 'Never mention Honour,' cries the Aunt. 'It becomes not the Mouth of such a Wretch. I am sorry, Niece, you force me to use these Words; but I cannot bear your grovelling Temper; you have none of the Blood of the Westerns in you.' (*TJ* 789)

Different versions of 'family honour' imply equally venal courses of action to Squire Western and his sister: is it honorable for a father to imprison his daughter, or for an aunt to take bribes from an aristocratic suitor?

As Nightingale's father says, 'Honour is a Creature of the World's Making' (*TJ* 690). Definitions vary according to class as well as interest: honour means propriety to the bourgeois Mrs Miller, while to Lady Bellaston honour has nothing to do with acts, but simply with disclosure and reputation. To a soldier, honour is martial: after Ensign Northerton assaults Tom, the lieutenant urges him to a duel. How can a Christian bear malice, asks Tom, when Christ has forbidden it? 'Why I believe there is such a Command,' cries the Lieutenant' 'but a Man of Honour can't keep it' (*TJ* 349). To the King of the Gypsies, the service of his people is true 'honour': to his subjects the cruellest punishment for misdemeanour is shame itself. Towards the end of the novel the word echoes through scene after scene, so that Fielding can deploy simple phrases like 'upon my honour' or 'do me the honour' with resonant irony and significance.

The chameleon usage implies a world where values are so relative that judgement is never easy: we must weave our way between conflicting codes. Circumstances, habits, and motives matter, and we cannot, like Square, regard 'virtue as a matter of theory only'. Readers of the novel, like the characters within it, have to distinguish convenient fictions or mindless habits from valid principles. Some judgements are easy – Blifil, Square, Thwackum, Lady Bellaston – but what are we to make of Black George, who steals from Tom yet is 'a true friend to him'? Or the highwayman who steals to feed his family? Or even Lord Fellamar, who plans to rape Sophia and press-gang Tom, but who struggles all night between 'appetite and honour'?

One of the fascinations of *Tom Jones* is that any single moral conclusion can seem at once accurate, yet inadequate. The headlong, humorous tone comes from Fielding's deliberate writing about 'mixed' humanity. By this he means not merely that he will write about varied worlds, from high life to low, but that within individuals good qualities overlay bad, and vice versa: as he says, 'there are no infallible individuals in this fiction'. It was this mixture, especially in the hero, that made the novel so disturbing to Dr Johnson, who felt that young people read books as 'Lectures of Conduct and Introductions into Life':

> Many writers, for the sake of following Nature, so mingle good and
> bad Qualities in their principal Personages, that they are both
> extremely conspicuous; and as we accompany them through their
> Adventures with Delight and are led by Degrees to interest ourselves
> in their Favour, we lose the Abhorrence of the Faults, because they do
> not hinder our Pleasure, or perhaps, regard them with some Kindness
> for being united with so much Merit.[4]

Fielding's aim, however, is precisely this: in his tracing of the
shifting meanings of honour, as of other terms like 'liberty' or
'justice', he depicts the complexity of the world, and the difficulty
of forming judgements. The techniques he employs to guide us are
both schematic and realistic. With his major characters, Tom and
Sophia, he makes clear what the 'mixture' is, and directs our
judgement. A second level of characters mingles diagrammatic
types – Blifil, Thwackum, Square, and Allworthy – with those
based on exaggerated characteristics (as in his drama) like Lady
Bellaston, Squire, and Mrs Western, or Mrs Miller. All are
strategically 'fixed', even caricatured, because they must play a
vital part, not only in the plot, but in the abstract argument. Finally,
through the intricate shading of minor characters – one of the
features that makes his fiction so distinctive – Fielding can make us
twist and turn to show exactly how difficult true judgement is. A
typical example is the landlady who first cossets Tom, because she
thinks he is rich, then, having wheedled his story out of him
becomes rude and cold because she learns he is a penniless
bastard: the reader's initial liking turns to disapproval. After she
churlishly refuses to cook him supper, she changes her mind: 'she
was really no ill-humoured woman at the Bottom' (*TJ* 373) but just
loved money and hated poverty; so we readjust our views again.
Finally, at the end of the chapter, we make a further revision, when
she explains her kindness, 'for many of these Bye-blows become
great Men, and, as my Husband used to say, never affront any
Customer that's a Gentleman' (*TJ* 376). In such small ways, the
reader's active judgement is demanded, tested, and refined.

We are also made aware of the inadequacy of legal 'judgement'
through the mistaken decisions of magistrates like Western, or
even Allworthy. The latter is a good man whose decisions are
impeccable when he knows the facts and the motives of those
involved. But his trusting nature, good will, and lack of

calculation make him easily duped by appearance and arguments, especially when these are cleverly geared (like Blifil's) to echo his own values. As readers, Fielding insists, we see behind the scenes: we can therefore judge better than Allworthy but should not judge *him* as too much at fault. The whole novel insists that – like the King of the Gypsies – we should query all outward appearances, and look behind them for previous history and hidden intent.

When all the circumstances are known, however, and we can judge the issue clearly, what principles should govern our sentencing? Among the gypsies, the shame of exposure itself is sufficient punishment. But is it practical, or right, to extend this to the community at large: the gypsies are an idealized community, providing the counterpoint of the 'noble savage' to the 'real', civilized world. On realistic terms, Tom's forgiveness of Black George at the end is condemned by Allworthy, speaking both as a Justice of the Peace, concerned with suppression of crime, and as a private man formulating values that bind society.

> 'Child,' cries Allworthy, 'you carry this forgiving Temper too far. Such mistaken Mercy is not only Weakness, but borders on Injustice, and is very pernicious to Society, as it encourages Vice. The Dishonesty of this Fellow I might perhaps have pardoned, but never his Ingratitude.' (TJ 862)

Yet Tom knows that mistakes are human, that circumstances can be desperate, that one act of kindness can outweigh a lifetime of misdoing. We must forgive each other and ourselves. When he begs forgiveness of Sophia, she suggests that he pass justice on himself, and decree his own sentence: ' " Alas Madam," answered he, "it is Mercy and not Justice which I implore at your Hands"' (TJ 864).

Justice is judgement by rules, mercy is the prerogative of the heart. In the opening chapters of Books XI and XIII, listing the principles that should guide an author, Fielding includes invention (based on observation), judgement, learning (for perspective as well as style), 'Conversation', a knowledge of all kinds of people that comes from wide experience. But all these tenets, he says, are nothing unless his 'Historian' has 'a good Heart and be capable of Feeling' (TJ 439). He must weep and laugh with his characters if he is to make his reader do so.

Concentration on Fielding's intellectual and philosophical themes tends to overlook his stress on sympathy and his own manipulation of the reader's emotion: none of the 'lessons' of the book would take hold if we did not share Sophia's love for Tom, and feel ready to forgive him.

Such tolerance, however, is sharply at odds with the realities of eighteenth-century Britain, and Fielding knows it. Although the book is firmly grounded in the real, showing how the world really works, in inns and drawing-rooms, hovels and prisons, its resolution is proudly *un*-realistic, asserting an ideal. In the 'real' world, Sophia's refusal of her father's wishes and her midnight flight could have led to her ruin; Tom, having lost his money and Allworthy's good will, could well have ended as a male prostitute or been hung for his part in the affray with Fitzpatrick. And even if their situation had been unravelled, Black George would still be condemned.

Fielding did not disdain such realism. It was exactly this direct, compassionate confronting of misery and vulnerable innocence that he admired in *Clarissa* in contrast to the 'dishonest' *Pamela*. He wrote generously to Richardson of his tears at Clarissa's despair: 'her letter to Lovelace is beyond any thing I have ever read. God forbid that the Man who reads this with dry Eyes should be alone with my Daughter when she hath no Assistance within Call ... It is well for the Critick that my Heart is now writing and not my Head.'[5] But he himself preferred to teach through laughter, not tears, as he says in his Dedication, employing 'all the Wit and Humour of which I am Master ... to laugh Mankind out of their Follies and Vices' (*TJ* 38). While *Tom Jones* hangs on the verge of the pit, never denying the existence of bailiffs, tyrants, rapists, oppressive fathers, we are secure in the knowledge that the plot will whisk us back from the brink.

The harsh facts of the 'world' are stated in the opening chapter of Book XV:

> There are a Set of Religious, or rather moral Writers, who teach that Virtue is the certain Road to Happiness, and Vice to Misery, in this World. A very wholsome and comfortable Doctrine, and to which we have but one Objection, namely, That it is not true. (*TJ* 695)

This is qualified by the belief – asserted in *Jonathan Wild* and *Amelia* – that private virtue is rewarded in this world: a clear conscience brings inner peace, while guilt brings inner torment. 'Public' virtue, however, inevitably falls prey to backbiting, contempt, and poverty. Yet the withdrawal and misanthropy of the Man on the Hill are not the answer. Recognition of evil must not devalue good. The fact that forgiveness and the pursuit of the happiness of others are at present only attainable in an 'untrue' fiction makes them all the more important to fight for. The finale enacts the benevolence that the whole novel recommends. With the magic three wishes of fiction Fielding salves the evil and despair that he saw every day as a magistrate, when he had no resource but inflexible codes of Law. In *Tom Jones* he applies to the world the subversive judgements that Minos applies in Elysium, in *A Journey from This World to the Next*.

Some critics, like Battestin, see *Tom Jones* as a typical example of Augustan neo-Christian didacticism. In this reading, on the grand scale, the plot traces the workings of *Providentia*, the Grand Design by which all things ultimately work to the general good. On the individual scale, it teaches *Prudentia*, the clear judgement we must acquire before gaining Wisdom – *Sophia*. Yet Fielding himself uses both 'Providence' and 'Prudence' in a characteristically sly fashion. When Allworthy learns from Nightingale senior that Black George has £500, for example:

> Here an Accident happened of a very extraordinary Kind; one indeed of those strange Chances, whence very good and grave Men have concluded that Providence often interposes in the Discovery of the most secret Villany, in order to caution Men from quitting the paths of Honesty, however warily they tread in those of Vice. (*TJ* 819)

In the ironic commentary, as in Fielding's other works, events are more often credited to accident or Fortune – a malign Goddess who takes pleasure in tormenting humans. It is the characters, not the all-seeing author, who credit providence, as Tom jokingly does for his being on the spot when he rescues the Man on the Hill; as Mrs Waters insists that 'Heaven seemed to have designed him as the happy Instrument of her Protection' (*TJ* 441); as Blifil cites 'the secret Direction of Providence', when trying to prove to Allworthy that Tom is 'one of the greatest Villains upon Earth' (*TJ* 788–9). This nicely suggests that Blifil will be hoist with his own 'providential' petard, but even dozing readers, constantly nudged by authorial interventions, can see that it is not providence, accident, or fortune, but the neat, outrageous dovetailing of plot that brings Tom to the rescue, or manœuvres Blifil's downfall.

Fielding did maintain an underlying belief in a benign universal order, but his providential fiction cleaves to an aesthetic and moral ideal or order, not a metaphysical one. It is only partly with tongue in cheek that he declares,

> This Work may, indeed, be considered as a great Creation of our own; and for a little Reptile of a Critic to presume to find Fault with any of its Parts, without knowing the Manner in which the Whole is connected, and before he comes to the final Catastrophe, is a most presumptuous Absurdity. (*TJ* 467)

This is how the world ought to be – the Grand Design and Gospel according to Fielding – not how it actually is. Furthermore, it is noticeable that Fielding's brand of providence almost always operates against the dictates of prudence, whether it be cautious self-interest or calculation of consequence. Indeed, 'prudent' is nearly always a sneer, and is Blifil's leading principle. Tom is foolish to act with complete disregard for how his actions will appear, but when Allworthy says he must learn prudence, he presents it as a defensive technique rather than a positive quality. When a man builds the foundation of his own ruin by indiscretion, he says, others will quickly build upon it, so 'Prudence is indeed the Duty which we owe to ourselves' (*TJ* 853).

Sophia's case is rather different: her actions are unequivocally 'right' in Fielding's eyes, whereas Tom's are often 'wrong'. Yet her instinctive wisdom operates in defiance, not only of the intemperate Squire but of the more worldly Mrs Western. The latter delivers many 'Lectures of Prudence' to Sophia,

> recommending to her the Example of the Polite World, where Love (so the good Lady said) is at present entirely laughed at, and where Women consider Matrimony, as Men do Offices of public Trust, only as the Means of making their Fortunes, and advancing themselves in the World. (*TJ* 292)

Much later as she prepares to press the suit of Lord Fellamar, she introduces her theme, Fielding says acidly, 'by some prefatory Discourse on the Folly of Love, and on the Wisdom of legal Prostitution for Hire' (*TJ* 769). A prudent marriage is a loveless, worldly one. The virtue becomes inverted: to preserve herself, Sophia must be imprudent, on a grand scale.

This inversion is typical of popular art, a strong element in much of Fielding's work. *Tom Jones* is a lesson in worldly judgement which is also a fairy-tale; a Bunyanesque fable of the loss and regaining of Paradise Hall; a parable in which the Prodigal Son turns out to be the true, loving, heir. The wisdom of these ancient folk-forms is paradoxical, often at odds (as in *King Lear*) with the conventional wisdom of the world. ('Wise' in Fielding, is usually as pejorative as 'prudent'.) The charmed figures follow their innate nature, acting on impulse and instinct. They speak out, they give to the undeserving, they make rash, courageous gestures. While the world rewards guile, calculation, and exploitation, they win the prize through openness, boldness, and compassion.

3

The pleasures of *Tom Jones* are manifold, enhanced by the marvellous three-part movement. The slow first six books set the scene and establish the values; the central six on the road are packed with pursuits, encounters, and intricate collisions; the final six spin to a close in London. Towards the end the action is orchestrated with a musical or mathematical inevitability, as one by one all the characters are drawn inexorably to the city. The revelations of the past resolve the crisis of the present, culminating in the dance of harmony, the final mock-Shakespearian circle of marriages.

The bravura inclusiveness of Fielding's comic vision is perhaps best illustrated by his brilliant invention of Squire Western – swearing and roaring, childish and dangerous, dancing with glee when he thinks Tom is to be hung, then pushing him into Sophia's arms and cooing over their baby. Fielding employs every type of comedy – of language, misunderstanding, farce, character, satire and sentiment – with supreme confidence. But he is also experimental, determined that the form, like the content, of his 'prosai-comic-epic' will shed old, empty rules. The opening chapters to each book, ironic but serious, test principles for the manipulation of time (II), the use of stylistic embellishments (IV), the importance of contrast (V), the role of the omniscient author in guiding judgement (VII), the conjunction of the 'marvellous' with realism.

Occasionally the voice is tart, as when he attacks the critics (XI). Sometimes it sounds haughty, as when he writes of love (VI). But even here, where he seems to exclude, Fielding is equally self-exposing and embracing. At the start of the novel he invites his readers in by offering his mixed bill of fare – not as for a private dinner, but as a public house open to all. But while he wants them to consume and enjoy, he also demands that they participate, learn how to 'read', and join a quest for standards of judgement and principles of love. As he nears the end, he acknowledges that we have shared a long, demanding journey with him, and with his characters. Like travellers sharing a coach on the road, sighting their goal and abandoning their bickering, he asks us to mount into the 'Vehicle' of his fiction with 'Cheerfulness and Good-Humour; since, after this one Stage, it may possibly happen to us, as it commonly happens to them, never to meet more' (*TJ* 813).

6

Prison Gates: The *Enquiry* and *Amelia*

1

In July 1748 Henry Fielding became Justice of the Peace for Westminster, and in 1749 for Middlesex. His court was on the ground floor of his house in Bow Street, so he was still working and living in the area between Soho and the Strand, one of the most crowded and poverty-stricken districts of the capital. Magistrates of the day took an active role outside the court in detection of crime and maintenance of public order, but public provision of money and manpower was derisory. In *Amelia* (1751) Fielding laments the 'decrepit' and stupid watchmen, the fatuous constables, and the vicious magistrates like Thrasher. In reaction he was ferociously committed to reform such practices, working with his clerk, Joshua Brogden, with Saunders Welch, High Constable of Holborn, and, from January 1751, with his blind brother John, who joined him on the Westminster bench.

Fielding's adversaries cackled at the transformation of the well-known debtor and author of 'the adventures of footmen, and the lives of thief-catchers' into a Justice of the Peace.[1] In particular they pointed to his patronage by the Duke of Bedford and his friends in the Ministry. That his position as magistrate could never be wholly dissociated from politics was shown by two major incidents in 1749: the execution of a Devonshire man, Bosavern Penlez, and the Westminster by-election. Penlez was hanged for looting after a three-day riot in June, fomented by sailors who claimed to have been cheated at a brothel. Because he was a minor offender, committed for trial on the highly dubious evidence of the owner of the Star brothel, it was claimed that Fielding was in the pay of the pimps. The case was constantly cited by political opponents during

71

the by-election that November, when Fielding certainly supported the ministerial candidate, Viscount Trentham, hosting feasts for potential voters, and being accused of deliberately releasing the ringleader of a disruptive pro-Trentham gang. Mud sticks, but there is no evidence that Fielding abused his position. His strongest weapon was still his pen, and a spoof pamphlet prompted by the by-election, the *Covent-Garden Journal*, would give its name to his last, and best, weekly newspaper in 1752.

In January 1749, when Fielding was elected Chairman of the Westminster Quarter Sessions, his address *A Charge to the Grand Jury* was a call for moral as much as legal reform. He asked citizens to be 'Censors of the Nation' (*E*. 29), rooting out the evils which engendered crime: blasphemy and political disaffection, indecency, brothel-keeping, gaming-houses, and masquerades. All these were blamed as pernicious and pervasive, symptoms of chronic diseases, 'which have so inveterated themselves in the Blood of the Body Politic, that they are perhaps never to be totally ineradicated' (*E*. 14). If he could not cure them, the magistrate's duty was to 'palliate and keep down' such ills (*E*.14).

Such bodily metaphors, typical of civic humanist pronouncements, pervade Fielding's legal writing. They creep into *Amelia*, too – for example, when the good Dr Harrison receives a caustic riposte from a nobleman to his 'obsolete and long exploded' notions that men should be promoted on grounds of merit, not influence: ' "This is all mere *Utopia*," cries his Lordship. "The chimerical system of Plato's republic with which we amused ourselves at University; Politics which are inconsistent with the State of Human Affairs" ' (*A*. 467). Does not Dr Harrison realize that Britain is now a hopelessly corrupt nation?

> 'And would you think of governing such a People by the strict Principles of Honesty and Morality?'
>
> 'If it be so corrupt,' said the Doctor, 'I think it is high Time to amend it. Or else it is easy to foresee that *Roman* and *British* Liberty will have the same Fate; for Corruption in the Body Politic as naturally tends to Dissolution as in the Natural Body.' (*A*. 467–8)

Fielding still clung to the old view of society as an organic whole, in which the 'Constitution' meant far more than the legal entity. In his devastating tract *An Enquiry into the Causes of the Late Increase of Robbers* (published in 1751, the same year as *Amelia*) he defines the constitution as including the fundamental laws and the legislative, executive, and municipal provisions, but also 'the Customs, Habits and Manners of the People. These, joined together, do, I apprehend, form the Political, as the several Members of the Body, the animal Oeconomy, with the Humours and Habit, compose that which is called the Natural Constitution' (*E.* 65). Understanding of *people* is therefore as vital to a law-maker or judge as technical knowledge.

The metaphor of the body alternates with that of society as a family, or rather an estate, with a benign master (under the law) in charge of his family, tenants, labourers, and servants. But, as the cynical lord in *Amelia* pointed out, he was applying outdated models. Both the novel and the *Enquiry* show Fielding struggling to reconcile his ideal of a hierarchical society, bound by *moral* laws, with his realistic perception of it as a commercial entity, bound by *economic* laws. The *Enquiry*, indeed, has been called 'the most extended example of the conflict between humanistic and Mandevillian accounts of the hierarchy'.[2] Thus he claims that all 'Philosophers' would find that trade has changed the values of the nation for the worse, especially those of the 'lower Sort', turning 'the Simplicity of their Manners into Craft; their Frugality into Luxury; their Humility into Pride, and their Subjection into Equality' (*E.* 70). But this is immediately followed by the admission that 'Politicians' (as opposed to philosophers) will find compensations for these 'moral Evils', since wealth has undoubtedly increased 'the Grandeur and Power of the Nation', fostering arts and sciences and improving the material quality of life (*E.* 70). His concern is not to attack wealth and privilege, but to castigate the way the aristocratic ethos of 'luxury' filters into the general populace, encouraging greed, idleness, and crime.

At first then, the *Enquiry* seems to strike a very different note from the humane tolerance of *Tom Jones*. For example, one of Fielding's remedies for disorder is fear. His passionate plea for private executions is not aimed at the inhumanity of public spectacles like Tyburn, but at the way they dignify criminals, arousing 'the Compassion of the Meek and tender-hearted, and the Applause, Admiration, and Envy of all the bold and hardened' (*E.* 167). But a tone of horror and pity rings through the final lines of his treatise, at the way 'many Cart-loads of our Fellow-creatures are once in six weeks carried to Slaughter', especially when, with proper Care and Regulations, much the greater part of these Wretches might have been made not only happy in themselves, but very useful Members of the Society. Upon the whole, something should be, Nay, must be done... not only Care for Public Safety, but common Humanity, exacts our Concern on this Occasion. (*E.* 172)

Despite Fielding's conservatism, the *Enquiry* was humane, realistic, and unusually progressive in linking crime to poverty, separating the despairing acts of the starving, disabled, and insane, from deliberate criminal activity. It attacks the current poor laws, and (like Hogarth's engraving *Gin Lane*, published only a month earlier) calls for action to reduce the widespread drunkenness which underlay much crime. Both here and in *Amelia* – rightly called the first English social protest novel – Fielding suggests that perjury, and handling of stolen goods (by which powerful dealers incited those less fortunate to commit crimes), be treated as felony. In practice as well as in theory, as a magistrate he carefully weeded out the victims of circumstance from the true malefactors, giving money for a market-stall to a woman 'guilty of no crime but poverty', dismissing charges against a mother of three small children charged 'with a paultry Larceny of a Cap value 3d' (*CGJ* 409), and avoiding sending young girls to Bridewell. He was still an optimist, who believed that it was possible, and obligatory, to try to right wrongs.

One other practical venture ran alongside his magistrate's work. This was the Universal Register Office, founded with his brother John in February 1749, an agency which tackled everything from money-lending and employment to insurance, estate management, and travel. The motive was profit, but the justification was still framed in terms of a hierarchical yet mutually co-operative community: if no talent was unwasted and no want unrelieved, then 'Society might be said to have attained its utmost Perfection' (*CGJ* 3).

The Universal Register, the dedicated work in court, and the firm campaigning tracts suggest an unstoppable energy. But Fielding's writings have an embattled note, reflecting the grinding impossibility of the magistrate's task. His spirits were also lowered by a sad string of deaths: his baby daughter Mary Amelia, born in January 1749, died that December; his sister Catharine and his 8-year-old son Henry, in 1750; two other sisters, Ursula and Beatrice, in early 1751. All were probably victims of a virulent fever epidemic.

Although Fielding and Mary had another daughter, Sophia (born 1750), and were able to escape to Bath and Somerset, Henry was increasingly ill, with gout and rheumatic disorders. He never lost his love of a good joke, and a good meal, and a good friend, but he was almost crippled and in constant pain. A guest at Ralph Allen's saw 'a poor, emaciated worn-out rake, whose gout and infirmities have got the better even of his buffoonery', while his friend Edward Moore blamed earlier intemperance: 'Fielding continued to be visited for his sins so as to be wheeled about from room to room.'[3] It was hard not to feel that his own body, like the body of the state, was paying for its unbridled appetites. *Amelia*, begun in 1749 and worked on intensively in 1751, was not the joyous comedy that everyone was waiting for, but the work of the battling magistrate and the repentant man.

2

Amelia is a brilliant, dismaying novel in which Fielding's flashing irony seems baffled, caught in a maze, like his protagonists. It is a novel about deception, and in the end it seems wilfully to deceive its reader, as if the romantic resolution does not spring from within, as it does in *Tom Jones*, but is almost forced on the plot from without. In a way this is in keeping with the whole tenor of the book: one can no longer trust that virtue brings its own reward, even in a fictional world.

If Charlotte Fielding is resurrected in all her vitality as Sophia, here, as Amelia, she haunts the text like a wronged ghost. Images foreshadowing this novel can be found in *Tom Jones*, where Western watches Sophia weeping with no more contrition or remorse than a Newgate turnkey or where her aunt rejects her pleas with the stony indifference of a bailiff to a debtor: 'in vain the wretched Captive attempts to raise Compassion; in vain the tender Wife bereft of her Companion, the little prattling Boy or frighted Girl, are mentioned as Inducements to Reluctance' (*TJ* 306). Fielding had dealt with the disruption of a family through unjust imprisonment before, in *Jonathan Wild*, but there Heartfree was an innocent victim whereas here Billy Booth is partly to blame. This is the kind of guilt, and the kind of misery, that Fielding deliberately keeps out of *Tom Jones*, confining it to simile or to the 'exemplary' story of the Man on the Hill:

> 'To see a Woman you love in Distress; to be unable to relieve her, and at the same Time to reflect that you have brought her to this Situation, is, perhaps, a Curse of which no Imagination can represent the Horrors to those who have not felt it.' 'I believe it from my soul,' cries *Jones*: 'and I pity you from the bottom of my Heart.' He then took two or three disorderly turns about the Room, and at last begged Pardon and flung himself into a Chair, crying, 'I thank Heaven I have escaped that.' (*TJ* 408–9)

Booth does not escape. During one crisis, when Amelia blames 'the barbarous World' for her husband's ruin, her little daughter asks who might hurt 'poor Papa'. Has he done any harm to anybody?

> 'No my dear Child,' said the Mother, 'he is the best Man in the World, and therefore they hate him.' Upon which the Boy, who was extremely sensible for his Years, answered, 'Nay, Mamma, how can that be? Have you not often told me that if I was good, every body would love me?' 'All good People will,' answered she. 'Why don't they love Papa then?' replied the Child, 'for I am sure he is very good.' 'So they do, my dear,' said the Mother, 'but there are more bad People in the world, and they will hate you for your Goodness.' (*A*. 161–2)

Stubbornly pursuing the logic of this, the son deduces that bad people are loved more than good. Amelia replies that the love of one good person is worth more than that of 'a thousand wicked ones', and then, as if to resolve all argument, concludes: 'Nay, if there was no such Person in the world, still you must be a good Boy: for there is one in Heaven who will love you; and his Love is better for you than that of all mankind' (*A*. 162).

In his commentary Fielding explicitly presents Amelia as a model mother, who annexes associations of shame to evil so that her children are entirely free of 'Pride, Envy, Malice'. But the passage is noteworthy for two other reasons. The first is the increasing bewilderment of the 'sensible' son (both 'sensitive' and rational) and the mother's final appeal to divine, not human, love. The second is the suspicion that Amelia is dishonest, or at least blindly self-deceiving. Booth *has* done someone harm – Amelia and his children. He is not hated for his goodness, but pursued for debts which result from his own recklessness. We are told to trust Amelia's judgement, yet we witness misjudgement. This is more than another instance of the innocent being unable to see evil (a constant theme of Fielding); it is typical of the ambivalent narration throughout. One feels that Fielding deliberately exploits the Richardsonian technique of immersion in experience to show how different accounts may be limited or subjective, or even deliberately angled for effect.

The opening of *Amelia* promises neutrality and bourgeois solemnity: 'The various Accidents which befel a very worthy Couple, after their uniting in the State of Matrimony, will be the Subject of the following History' (*A*. 13). The jesting, questioning, gentleman-author of Fielding's earlier fictions is to be banished. This impersonality is soon reinforced by a striking definition of the didactic function of the novel:

> By examining carefully the several Gradations which conduce to bring every Model to Perfection, we learn truly to know that Science in which the Model is formed: as Histories of this Kind, therefore, may properly be called Models of HUMAN LIFE; so, by observing minutely the several Incidents which tend to the Catastrophe or Completion of the Whole, and the minute Causes by which those Incidents are produced, we shall best be instructed in this most useful of all Arts, which I call the ART OF LIFE (*A*. 14)

To realize how original this is (although the word 'science' here retains its older meaning of 'knowledge' and 'principles') one must look forward a hundred years, to George Eliot's implied analogy in *Middlemarch* between the imagination of the novelist and the scientist: 'provisionally framing its object and correcting it to more and more exactness of relation: he wanted to pierce the obscurity of those minute thoroughfares which prepare human misery and joy'.[4]

The first problem in *Amelia*, then, for both characters and reader is one of perception and insight. First to see 'objectively' what is going on, and then to try to make sense of it. To convey the opacity of experience, and the subjectivity of perception and reporting (including this 'history'), Fielding makes a bold formal choice. Perhaps influenced by the emotional impact of *Clarissa*, he combines the fixed characters and symbolic incidents of his prose-epics (no longer so comic) – with the sentimental, detailed, bourgeois romance, altering its focus from quest and courtship to the 'bonds' of matrimony. The form shifts, sometimes uneasily, between allegorical satire and realism. The setting is confined: narrow alleys, apartments, courtrooms, bailiff's 'palaces' and

77

prisons, the 'Verge of the Court' where debtors could find sanctuary. The style, too, is closed in, cluttered with detail, of clothes, meals, rooms: the minutiae of experience parallel the 'minute' causes of action. The 'mixed' quality of individual psychology is fluid rather than schematic. The reversals and surprises are still there, but the focus is close-up and confusing. The old ironic distance is denied us.

A fundamental irony does remain, in the adaptation of epic to the squalor of London streets. This time, by Fielding's own account, the model is Virgil rather than Homer, but the mood is less mock-heroic than sub-heroic. The story is set in the early 1730s, and begins *in medias res*, with Booth's unjust arrest as he goes to help a man in a brawl, but instead of being introduced as the hero, he is merely one case that comes before the corrupt justice Thrasher: 'A young Fellow, whose name was Booth, was now charged with beating the Watchman' (*A*. 18). Since we have already seen three ignorant, prejudiced, miscarriages of justice, Booth's predicament is made to appear representative, rather than special. In Newgate prison, all normal expectations are confounded. The inversions here are relentlessly grim, far from the comic paradoxes of early works like *Joseph Andrews*. The hideous Blear-Eyed Moll attracts a 'very pretty young Fellow' (*A*. 21). Street-robbers due to be hanged laugh over a bottle. A minor felon learns that his pregnant wife has flung herself from a window. A daughter is condemned for stealing a loaf for her dying father, and the father condemned for receiving it. Language itself reels at the jarring juxtapositions: a beautiful girl, whose face speaks her innocence, hurls 'a Volley of Words, each one of which was too indecent to be repeated' (*A*. 25).

There is an aura of sexual assault as well as penal cruelty and indifference – in Moll's brutal advances, in the way a man gaoled for 'certain odious unmanlike Practices, unfit to be named' is given 'various Kinds of Discipline' by the prostitutes, which almost put his life at risk (*A*. 25). The setting casts a murky light over the shabby prison affair of Booth and Miss Matthews. In epic style, as a prelude to romance (a non-heroic variant of Dido and Aeneas in the cave), each tells his or her story. Miss Matthews relates her seduction, desertion, and attempt at murder. Booth describes his wooing of Amelia, the opposition of her mother and sister, their elopement, his service in Gibraltar, and their idyllic rural life until his debts brought him to London. Many elements in Booth's story will play a part in the rest of the book: the moral guidance of Dr Harrison; the 'good friend' Captain (later Colonel) James; the mixture of martial ferocity and brotherly tenderness in Colonel Bath. But we see them all through Booth's eyes, and, in this context, can we trust his narration? More confusing still, Booth mouths some of Fielding's own views, yet uses the empty, high-flown clichés which Fielding characteristically mocks, as in his assertion that benevolence is unrelated to station: 'In Reality, Palaces, I make no Doubt, do sometimes contain nothing but Dreariness and Darkness, and the Sun of Righteousness hath shone forth with all its Glory in a Cottage' (*A*. 118). Is Fielding being sly here, or straight?

I think it is quite possible, since the cunning author is so deliberately absent, that we are intended to read parts of *Amelia* with the same suspicious eyes as Fielding read *Pamela*. John Coolidge has suggested, for example, that Miss Bennett's history cloaks a story of stubborn self-interest beneath a lament of the trials of innocence.[5] In a similar way, we might suspect that Booth's account of his renunciation of Amelia on the grounds that he has no money, cleverly exploits the language of virtuous self-sacrifice to persuade Harrison, and Amelia's mother, that he is no fortune hunter. It is equally possible – although again this is never hinted – to read Booth's whole story of his former life as a deliberately Othello-like wooing of Miss Matthews, at once rousing her jealousy and modesty and letting her feel in control.

Judgement becomes problematic. Fielding tells us, for instance, that Booth is 'a Man of consummate Good-nature' (*A*. 145) and praises his capacity for affection and tenderness, but this accolade comes just as he is sliding towards adulterous sex with Miss Matthews. When the gaoler locks the couple in for the night, readers are asked to 'weigh attentively' all the circumstances. Booth is a young man, healthy, slightly drunk, lonely, faced with 'a fine young Woman' using all her arts to enflame (*A*. 148). Should we, as Amelia later does in her calm, un-dramatizing way, make 'large Allowances' (*A*. 508) and forgive him? Noticeably, the narrator refrains from comment. Further on, however, in a different context, Dr Harrison writes an eloquent letter on the way that adultery spreads misery, like waves, through the lives of all it touches.

Amelia herself does not appear until Book IV. After a week of 'criminal Conversation', Miss Matthews has just heard of her release and has paid to obtain Booth's liberty. She then asks for the prison account:

> The Governor was now approaching with a long Roll of Paper, when a faint Voice was heard to cry out hastily, 'where is he?' – and presently a female Spectre, all pale and breathless, rushed into the Room, and fell into Mr. *Booth's* Arms, where she immediately fainted away. (*A*. 153)

The conjunction of the long roll of paper – reminding us of the stories, the debts, and the scroll of judgement – with the sudden appearance of the spectre, as if conjured by Booth's guilty conscience, is bleakly ominous. Throughout there is something ghostly about Amelia, in her clean white gown. She has none of the realistic gutsiness of Sophia under stress, when 'her face was whiter than snow and her heart was throbbing through her stays' (*TJ* 646). This is not to say Amelia lacks strength – she is tough enough to elope (braving pouring rain as well as maternal anger); she is sweetly domesticated with her mutton hash and neat shifts; she can laugh at Mrs Ellison, be angry with Mrs Atkinson, feel attracted to the devoted Serjeant. She is prepared to pawn her belongings, and shows considerable courage, defying the mores of her class, when she declares she is prepared to work for a living. But she is constantly either the embodiment of domestic and religious pieties, or the object of male lust. Even at the end, when she learns of her restored inheritance, Amelia lays claim to no life of her own, thanking Heaven and embracing Booth, exclaiming, 'My dear Love, I wish you Joy: and I ought in Gratitude to wish it you; for you are the Cause of mine. It is upon yours, and my Children's account, that I principally rejoice.'

Part of the despairing quality of the book comes from a feeling that, on their own, Booth and Amelia could never overcome the 'barbarous World'. Fielding makes it clear that their plight is largely structural. As a half-pay officer who has left the army, Booth's one chance of earning money is to regain his commission. He has served with gallantry, but under the present system no weight is given to merit: 'boys' are placed in command and footmen are bought places, before deserving officers. The lottery of state preferment is no surer than the gaming tables. Booth is reliant on the intercession of others like the 'noble lord' and

Colonel James (both of whom plan to seduce Amelia, and thus suggest distant postings in the West Indies). Later, Captain Trent, pimping for both men, openly implies that Booth should prostitute his wife to save his family from starvation. Other powerful men require political or financial, rather than sexual payment. Dr Harrison's friend will only help if Harrison supports his candidate in an election. Another 'noble man' casually snaps up Booth's last £50, carefully scraped together by Amelia – a naturally expected 'touching', defined as 'the modern Methods of Business' (*A*. 483), which equates these payments to hierarchy with the automatic bribing of Newgate gaolers.

Since all institutions are equally corrupt, the good are faced with a practical ethical problem of ends and means. When Mrs Atkinson, disguised as Amelia, pretends to accept the noble lord's favours, she gains a commission for her husband at the cost of jeopardizing her friend's reputation. Fielding presents this as wrong, but also understandable. The novel's sexual dealings mirror the financial, professional, and political chicanery: men's desires prey on and infect the body of the women just as they exploit and corrupt the body politic. The 'noble lord', who seduces for mere novelty (and passes venereal disease to Mrs Bennett), is the sexual equivalent of the 'great man' who snaps up Booth's bribe:

> The great Man received the Money, not as a Gudgeon doth a Bait, but as a Pike receives a poor Gudgeon into his Maw. To say the Truth, such Fellows as these may well be likened to that voracious Fish, who fattens himself by devouring all the little Inhabitants of the river. (*A*. 483)

Since no one voluntarily jumps into the pike's jaws, deception (as in the Art of Thriving) is an essential skill: people must be tricked into self-destruction. Disguise, masks, and masquerades are key images in this book. When Amelia is young, and breaks her nose, she wears a mask: removing it, guiltily fascinated by the possibility of her disfigurement, Booth falls in love with her. He is won not by her beauty (as Terry Castle notes, Fielding elliptically avoids saying what she looks like), but, it seems, almost by the act of revelation. In London, everyone wears a mask: removed, it displays their ugliness, provoking not love, but dismay. In all cases, however, despite Amelia's innocence, it seems that masks are a means of entrapment. The lord appears at the oratorio in an eye-patch and shabby clothes to catch Amelia; the bailiff dresses as a woman to catch a debtor.

The metaphor finds its fullest expression in the masquerade at Ranelagh. Amelia stays at home, having changed places with Mrs Atkinson; Mrs James goes, having changed her disguise. Both women thus trick their husbands, although their motives are very different. Mrs James learns the truth about her marriage, when she talks with the 'shepherdess', Miss Matthews; Booth believes falsehoods about his, when he sees his supposed 'wife' with the noble lord. Truth and lies intermingle: edges blur. This confusion extends to the reader, since Fielding refuses to identify the characters beneath the dominoes, and one has to re-read (in all senses) to sort out who is who, and what is happening. There is something exhilarating as well as disturbing about the writing, as though Fielding's disapproval itself 'masks' an ambivalent attraction to the subversive energy of the masquerade with its dangerous blurrings of class and identity, its complex couplings, its formal dance of misrule.

The bafflement of masks is like the rat-run of streets, the topsy-turvy rules of Newgate, or the illogical laws of the nation. Towards the end of the book the good Justice sighs wearily: 'to speak my Opinion plainly, such are the Laws, and such the Method of Proceeding, that one would almost think the Laws were rather made for the Protection of Rogues, than for the Punishment of them' (A. 493).

What philosophy can explain the prison of the world, and sustain those trapped in it? Fielding raises the issue ironically in the opening description of his worthy couple: 'the Distresses which they waded through were so exquisite, and the Incidents which produced them so extraordinary, that they seemed to require not only the utmost Malice, but the utmost Intervention which Superstition has ever attributed to Fortune' (A. 14). But, he asks, do we not attribute too much to this capricious deity? Should we not rather look to 'natural causes', both for the roots of misery, and the efforts by which the good overcome it?

At times the novel has the air of a Socratic debate, as, one by one, different characters pronounce on this question. The argument begins in Newgate, where the Free-thinker, Robinson, who denies the existence of divine Providence, recommends stoical indifference: 'for what is is, and what must be, must be' (A.

22). Yet at the end Robinson's confession of a forged will becomes the 'providential' means by which Amelia's fortune is restored: the Booths' initial predicament sprang not from Fate, but from the 'natural' greed of Amelia's sister, and her lawyer Murphy. A second Newgate view is offered by a Methodist, who declares crime to be mere human error and not necessarily evil: 'nay, perhaps the worse a Man is by Nature, the more Room there is for Grace' (*A.* 27). Yet another theory is put forward by Miss Matthews, who follows 'that charming fellow Mandevil' in arguing that human nature is fundamentally rapacious: the words virtue and religion 'serve only as Cloaks under which Hypocrisy may be better enabled to cheat the World' (*A.* 108).

In these opening chapters Booth is depicted as an agnostic, holding that events are ruled by chance and actions by 'ruling passions', a refinement of the theory of humours. He agrees with Robinson on the 'Necessity of Human Actions' but rejects the idea that we are victims of blind impulse or fate, insisting 'that every Man acted merely from the force of that Passion which was uppermost in his Mind, and could do no other' (*A.* 24). As double victims of accident and feeling, we cannot be held responsible for our actions. But ruling passions can range from revenge and lust to benevolence and pity, so when Miss Matthews quotes Bernard de Mandeville, Booth combats her cynicism by pointing that Mandeville's system omits love, man's 'best Passion' (*A.* 108).

The novel often seems to support Miss Matthews. Most codes – bourgeois or aristocratic – turn out to be either self-interested or inhumane, whether it be the bailiff's mercantile pragmatism or Colonel Bath's code of honour. Both devalue human life, and Fielding links them with a simile. Mr Bondum the bailiff is 'an honest and good Man in his Way' who bears no malice to the 'Bodies' in his care, but simply wants to acquire bail-bonds, like a butcher dividing a carcass into as many joints as possible: 'As to the Life of the Animal, or the Liberty of the Man, they are Thoughts which never obtrude themselves on either' (*A.* 317). Colonel Bath is also honest, unfailingly tender to his sister, 'a perfect good Christian except in the articles of Fighting and Swearing' (*A.* 521). Yet he will fight a duel at the merest whiff of offence, making 'no more of cutting the Throat of a Man upon any of his Punctilio's than a Butcher doth of killing Sheep.'

Dr Harrison attacks duelling with vigour, setting it against the tenets of Christianity. In the absence of an ironic, intervening author, Harrison is our moral mentor. His letter on adultery is jeeringly read aloud by the Ranelagh rakes. He argues with a young clergyman on forgiveness, vengeance, and just punishment; he lectures on respect for the clergy, on the palace of God as superior to the court of Kings, on the way that neglect of merit corrupts the body politic. His speeches bulge with untranslated quotations, as if Fielding was using him to conduct an academic debate detached from the action: his teasing of Mrs Atkinson about Homer and Virgil is not just a dig at female learning (always irresistible) but a demonstration of the importance of reading authorities accurately. Harrison certainly speaks for Fielding when he tells Amelia fiercely, in the face of all the evidence, that all men are not 'almost Villains in their Hearts'.

> 'Fie, Child,' cries the Doctor. 'Do not make a Conclusion so much to the Dishonour of the great Creator. The Nature of Man is far from being in itself Evil: It abounds with Benevolence, Charity and Pity, coveting Praise and Honour, and shunning Shame and Disgrace. Bad Education, bad Habits, and bad Customs, debauch our Nature and drive it headlong as it were into Vice. The Governors of the World, and I am afraid the Priesthood, are answerable for the Badness of it.' (*A*. 381)

This moves beyond a last-ditch defiance of the Hobbes-Mandeville view, to call for responsibility on the part of the 'great', a cry that echoes through the darkness of the novel as a whole.

In the end, however, it is not Harrison's solemn words, Amelia's unselfish acts, or the sudden turn of Fortune (or Providence) that persuade Booth into a trust in revealed religion. In prison he reads the sermons of Dr Barrow – and all his doubts vanish. Although the Revd Isaac Barrow (a great proponent of benevolence) was one of Fielding's favourite divines, this feels like a mechanical stroke. Booth's conversion is dispatched in two lines, quite without conviction, and is briskly reconciled to the theory of passions by Harrison's assertion that religion speaks to the strongest passions of all, 'Hope and Fear' (*A*. 522). At the end the Booths' happiness is restored and poetic justice ensures that miscreants meet appropriate horrid fates. But the conclusion still feels evasive and insecure. Although Booth escapes the city prison, its shadow still confines him: he 'returned into the County and hath never since been thirty Miles from home' (*A*. 545).

7

From Covent Garden to Lisbon

1

Amelia was admired by 'a judicious few' for its strong moral tone, and later by Dr Johnson, who liked it even better than *Clarissa*.[1] But many readers complained that Fielding had lost his comic touch. The good characters were dull, while the underworld settings were abominably 'low' and offensive to good taste. Having stayed clear of literary controversy for some time, Fielding had re-entered the fray by beginning a 'Paper War' in his new *Covent-Garden Journal* in January 1752. Old enemies were joined by new opponents, like the rebarbative critic John Hill, and Tobias Smollett (who thought Fielding had pinched the character of Partridge in *Joseph Andrews* from Strap in *Roderick Random*). To add to the humiliation, in the first edition Fielding had mentioned Amelia's injured nose, but not its mending: since a damaged nose was a sign of syphilis, critics had a field-day.

Pamphlets, satires, and comic verse rained down. Smarting under the onslaught, Fielding defended his novel movingly in a comic trial in the *Journal*. The 'Town' claims the book is:

> *very sad Stuff*; that Amelia herself is a *low* Character, a *Fool*, and a *Milksop*; that she is very apt to faint, and apt *to drink Water*, to prevent it ... That she *shews too much Kindness for her children*, and is too apt to *forgive the Faults of her Husband*... That she once mentions THE DEVIL, and as often as not swears BY HER SOUL. Lastly that she is a Beauty WITHOUT A NOSE, I say again WITHOUT A NOSE. All this we shall prove by many Witnesses. (*CGJ* 58)

In the following issue, 'a great Number of Beaus, Rakes, fine Ladies and formal Persons with bushy Wigs', push forward as witnesses when a 'grave Man' asks to be heard (*CGJ* 65). Describing Amelia as his 'favourite Child', not free from faults, but the product of loving labour, he suggests a compromise: 'I do, therefore, solemnly declare to you, Mr Censor, that I will trouble the World no more with any Children of mine by the same Muse' (*CGJ* 66).

Amelia was, indeed, Fielding's last novel. But the *Covent-Garden Journal* and *The Journal of a Voyage to Lisbon* show he had lost none of his flair. The *Covent-Garden Journal*, begun as an advertising medium for the Universal Register, ran for eleven months. Avoiding party politics, it contained a miscellany of news, and a report from Bow Street, compiled by the clerk Brogden. This was part of Fielding's attempt to control crime through example and information, but the Bow Street column shows his leniency as well as his strictness, and upset some readers by its humour (unsuitable to a court room) far more than by its catalogue of crime.

In the leading articles, Fielding writes as 'Sir Alexander Drawcansir, Knight, Censor of Great Britain', taking his persona from Buckingham's *Rehearsal* (the model for several of his plays). The name had already been applied to Fielding by Colley Cibber, who called him a 'Drawcansir in wit, who spared neither friend no foe'.[2] Once again, ridicule is his weapon and Lucian, Cervantes, and Swift are his models, writers who attacked folly and evil but, as he said, sent their satire laughing into the world. Fielding lacks Swift's scathing savagery, but his satirical rage is clear. For example, he deems Swift's *Modest Proposal* inadequate to solve the problem of London's poor: the Irish gentry might find local babies fed on milk and potatoes delicious, but, as London infants were almost wholly composed of gin, eating them might poison their consumers. Why not restore human sacrifice instead, providing a religious sanction for a political expedient?

The articles range from campaigning pieces – on gambling, duelling, prostitution, poverty, and religion – to satire and reviews. Friends like Hogarth and Kitty Clive are praised and feuds are kept up, as in the spirited account of the battle between Garrick at Drury Lane and John Rich at Covent Garden. But new talents are recognized too, with a sympathetic review of Charlotte Lennox's *The Female Quixote*. Criticism spirals into absurdity, in a wild parody of an editor of *Hamlet*, or the archaic artisan debating society 'The Robinhoodians'. And sometimes wit lurches happily into fatuous schoolboy silliness. Learned works, for example, previously lost through sword, fire, and the 'devouring Moths of Antiquity' (*CGJ* 47–8) are now held to be threatened by an application for which 'Parchment and Vellum, the antient repositories of Learning, would have been utterly unfit', but which is clearly indicated by advertisements for books printed *'on a superfine, delicate, soft Paper*, and again, *very proper to be had in all Families'*. Alas, the curious searcher into Antiquity hereafter 'will never be able to wipe off the Injuries of Time' (*CGJ* 48).

The *Covent-Garden Journal* is lit by high spirits, reforming energy, linguistic sharpness, and slapstick. The pace is always fast, and the best-known piece, 'A Modern Glossary', condenses Fielding's jibes at hypocrisy, frivolity, and self-interest into a bitter rush of terms. It begins with,

> ANGEL. The name of a Woman, commonly a very bad one.
> AUTHOR. A laughing Stock. It means likewise a poor Fellow and in
> general an Object of Contempt.

> (*CGJ* 35)

and ends thus:

> WORTH. Power. Rank. Wealth.
> WISDOM. The art of acquiring all three.
> WORLD. Your own acquaintance.

> (*CGJ* 38)

2

By these 'modern' definitions, our Author had no Worth and no Wisdom. But his World was wide. His acquaintance stretched from aristocrats and entrepreneurs, through political, legal, literary, and theatrical circles, to farmers and innkeepers, traders and vagrants. The latter took up many long hours, in court and out. Hoping to deter them from crime, he compiled a brief popular work, *Examples of the Interposition of Providence in the Detection and Punishment of Murder*, aimed at the sensation-loving public, and especially at children, already greedy for 'Tragical stories'. In court most of his cases were mundane, but that of Elizabeth Canning, who claimed to have been kidnapped and imprisoned in a brothel attic for a month, caught fashionable attention. She was later convicted of perjury, and Fielding, implicated in the faulty prosecution, wrote a pamphlet explaining his role: an all too real example of the difficulty of judging, and the credulity of over-trusting judges, that he had depicted in *Tom Jones*.

A more serious work, the *Proposal for Making an Effectual Provision for the Poor*, was submitted to the Prime Minister, Henry Pelham, in September 1752 and published the following January. Based on a detailed study of existing measures, it drew vivid pictures of the suffering London poor, in their 'Hunger, Cold, Nakedness and Filth' (*E.* 230), and suggested a radical solution: to shed the parish relief system and build vast complexes to house the poor of a whole county, providing employment as well as lodging. An architect's plan shows the proposed Middlesex 'County House' near Acton, to house 5,000 people, with 600 in a House of Correction. The scheme was relatively liberal compared to later Benthamite proposals, but it still sounds Draconian from a proclaimed champion of liberty, and a man so careful to distinguish the individual from the mass in his dealings on the bench. Fielding recognized this, but argued that, if one must 'on no account' deprive the poor of the liberty of

> doing what they will, going where they will, of Wandring and Drunkenness, why should we deny them that Liberty which is the Consequence of this; I mean that of Begging and Stealing, or Robbing and Cutting Throats at their good Pleasure. (*E.* 267)

Nothing came of the plan: the capital's poor grew poorer.

At the end of his tract, Fielding disarmed those who thought he coveted the role of a County House Governor. Despite the 'chearfulness which was always natural to me', he felt time was running out. He was suffering from jaundice, dropsy, and asthma; his muscles and flesh were wasting away. Searching for a cure, he visited doctors and quacks, tried every medicine including 'tarwater' and milk diets, and leased a farm at Fordhook, near Uxbridge, to get out of the London smoke. But he never stopped working. In August 1753, lame and 'very ill', planning a month's rest in Bath, he was kept in London by a request from the Duke of Newcastle for a plan to clear a recent rash of killings (five in one week). That autumn he set up a new system. News of a crime, reported to Bow Street or to any London turnpike, was passed immediately to a core of constables, backed by trained men. The basic idea, according to his brother John, was 'quick notice and sudden pursuit'. It worked: the cut-throat gangs were dispersed and the 'Bow Street Runners' became the forebears of the Metropolitan Police.

Fielding took pride in his success, but knew it had probably killed him. After a terrible winter and wet spring, a summer abroad was his last hope. In June he booked his passage for Lisbon on the *Queen of Portugal*. With him went his wife Mary, his 16-year-old daughter Harriet, only remaining child of his marriage to Charlotte, two servants, and Mary's friend Margaret Collier. The journey was constantly protracted, first by delays in setting out, then by contrary winds. The ship was forced to weigh anchor off Deal, off Ryde on the Isle of Wight (where Fielding stayed on shore for a week), and off Torbay (where he sent hogsheads of excellent cider to his London friends.) In all, the 'short' voyage took three weeks.

3

Fielding described his departure in *The Journal of a Voyage to Lisbon*. On the day he left Fordhook, he awoke to the 'most melancholy sun I have ever beheld', knowing he must say goodbye to his younger children, William, aged 6, Sophia, now 4, and the baby, Allen. Like Abraham Adams believing his son drowned, all his stoicism deserted him,

> In this Situation, as I could not conquer Nature, I submitted entirely to her, and she made as great a Fool of me as she had ever done of any Woman whatsoever; under Pretence of giving me leave to enjoy, she drew me in to suffer, the Company of my little ones during eight Hours; and I doubt not whether, in that Time, I did not undergo more than in all my Distemper. (*JL* 201)

The careful balance of conquest and submission, the personification of Nature as an internal version of the 'Fortune' which played such tricks with his fictional heroes, are symptomatic of the book. There is a constant tension between literary formality and personal confession, with Fielding as both controlling author and ambivalent 'hero'.

It is possible to be too serious about the *Journal*, which is, of its essence, an informal work. This does not mean that Fielding regarded it as unimportant, or took no pains with its composition, but the form is born of circumstance, not design. He began to write it out of boredom, stuck in his cabin off Deal: the polished author is confronted with unpolished, unfinished, and often uncomfortable reality. As if recognizing this, in his retrospective Preface he renounces imaginative models in favour of 'truthful' representation:

> in Reality, the Odyssey, the Telemachus, and all of that kind, are to the Voyage writing I here intend, what Romance is to true History, the former being the Confounder and Corrupter of the latter ... for my part, I must confess I should have honoured and loved Homer more had he written a true History of his own Times in humble Prose. (JL 185)

He also claims that his desire is to 'convey Instruction in a Vehicle of Entertainment; and so to bring about at once, like the Revolution in the *Rehearsal*, a perfect Reformation of the Laws relating to our maritime Affairs' (JL 189). But the mention of the *Rehearsal* signals a tongue-in-cheek, Drawcansir approach – and in the body of the journal itself maritime affairs are presented as almost uncontrollable; as the sea is opposite to the land, so sailors have differed from landsmen since the time of Homer and are an alien, self-governing species.

Fielding is, literally and metaphorically, at sea. 'Dead Luggage', unable to move, he is at the mercy of wave, wind, and other people. Doctors tap his stomach to drain fluid from his dropsy; watermen jeer as he is carried aboard; Captain Veal storms and raves; Mrs Francis presents her bills. At times his belief in human goodness, regardless of class, comes near to cracking. He even longs for the smooth hypocrisy of polite society: the cruel jeering of the watermen is 'an Excrescence of an uncontrolled Licentiousness mistaken for Liberty' (JL 202). Only a refined education can 'purge away that Malevolence of Disposition of which, at our Birth, we partake in common with the savage Creation' (JL 202).

The venom of the vulnerable appears too in his caricature of his landlady at Ryde, Mrs Francis (whom one feels may have suffered as much from Fielding's whims as he from hers). But here the tone is different. Although Claude Rawson is right to say that Fielding may have lost his Augustan balance and 'true Ease',[3] the portrait has a fierce zest in which the very act of writing is an affirmation of life and dominance. Fielding himself knows this. After 'writing-up' a play-like scene between the robustly complacent Captain and his self-important military nephew, he goes on to describe a storm, and his alarms for his family.

> Can I then say I had no Fear? Indeed I cannot. Readers, I was afraid for thee, lest thou should be deprived of that Pleasure thou art now enjoying; and that I should not live to draw out on Paper that military Character which thou didst peruse in the Journal of Yesterday. (*JL* 253)

The self-mocking joke has the ring of truth. Most authors experience that peculiar megalomaniac dread that they will die before people can read the work in progress, being dragged from the world, to borrow the poet Geoffrey Hill's words, 'Crying to the end "I have not finished"'. This transference of self to page is a recognition – a just one, in Fielding's case – that the writer's 'true' life persists in his words.

The *Journal*'s unevenness reveals Fielding's abundant, puzzled curiosity about people and the difficulty he feels when he cannot invent but must describe and respond in 'humble prose'. Some characters, like the acid and placid Mrs and Mr Francis, he can pin down: 'She was indeed as Vinegar to Oil, or a brisk Wind to a standing Pool' (*JL* 235). He forces them into 'types', as in Mr Francis's give-away answer to all questions, 'I don't know anything about it, Sir; I leaves all that to my Wife' (*JL* 235). Other characters prove more difficult. Captain Veal, for example, is nearly a Squire Western of the sea: an old pirate, roaringly superstitious, a greedy tyrant yet good to his sailors, and tender to the point of tears about animals. Fielding loves Veal's panic when a kitten is lost overboard, the dramatic rescue, the inanimate fluff on deck, slowly coming to life. But he frankly relishes the ironic coda, many pages later, 'when the Cat, which had shewn it could not be drowned, was found suffocated under a Featherbed in the Cabin. I will not endeavour to describe his Lamentations...' (*JL* 271). He wants to make the Captain pure paradox, a stage figure composed of rage and sentiment, generosity and selfishness: 'He was, moreover, a Man of Gallantry; at the Age of Seventy he had the Finicalness of Sir *Courtly Nice*, with the Roughness of *Surly*; and while he was deaf himself, had a Voice capable of deafening others' (*JL* 208). But sometimes Veal escapes him: the vitality of this 'character' is in its roughness, not its balance. Captain Veal stays half submerged, like a barnacled Atlantic reef.

The *Journal* is a witness, too, to Fielding's intensely physical response to life and his drive to translate the personal to the general. The familiar theme of food and appetite is reworked here in a continual contrast between his weak body and powerful hunger. Food is richness: venison at Ryde; clotted cream, sole and 'Whitings of almost preposterous size' in Devon (*JL* 262); a dire moment off Galicia when they are reduced to sea-biscuit, 'which I could not chew' (*JL* 280). The extension to the general comes in a swelling passage about the nutritious wealth of the ocean, and ends in a comic diatribe about the monopoly of London fishmongers, only to be abolished by hanging the lot – so we must change the law, to make 'starving thousands of Poor' into a felony (*JL* 264).

A similar physical response is felt in Fielding's excitement at the fleets of shipping on the Thames, and later in the Channel. Here too, as if personal enjoyment must be subordinate to communal good, these flow into reflections on trade, war, and patriotism. But nearing port at last Fielding basks in the moment, purely for itself. On a cloudless evening, all on board watch the dipping sun, and while the horizon is still 'blazing with Glory' they turn to see the full moon rising opposite: 'Compared to these, the Pageantry of Theatres, or Splendour of Courts, are Sights almost below the Regard of Children' (*JL* 279).

On 7 August, on a 'calm and moonshiny Night' (*JL* 284), the *Queen of Portugal* sailed up the Tagus. The white buildings of pre-earthquake Lisbon lined the banks, but, when they finally landed, after a day of wrangling with officials, Fielding was not enchanted. It seemed the 'nastiest City in the World', and they dashed through it to a coffee-house looking across the city to the sea, where they ate well, and were as 'well-charged as if the Bill had been made on the Bath-road between Newbury and London' (*JL* 285). Here, with that wry reminder of England, of the inns and the bills of *Joseph Andrews* and *Tom Jones*, Fielding could say, ' – *hic Finis chartaeque viaeque*' (*JL* 286). This is the end of the story, and the journey.

After a while the Fieldings and their entourage settled in the suburb of Junqueira. Life was hardly smooth: the servant William decamped with some of their money; the maid Bell also left; Margaret Collier infuriated Henry by setting her cap at his new friend, the clergyman John Williamson; Fielding even felt that Mary was conspiring against him. As matters calmed, he ordered new clothes from his tailor and sent generous presents home. But life was ebbing, and on 8 October 1754 he died. He was 47.

Henry Fielding was buried in the British cemetery, on a hill above Lisbon. A year later his cousin, Lady Mary Wortley Montagu, wrote that 'no man enjoyed life more than he did, though few had less reason to do so', since his highest public office involved 'raking in the lowest sinks of vice and misery', but:

> His happy constitution (even when he had, with great pains, half demolished it) made him forget everything when he was before a venison pasty or over a flask of champagne, and I am persuaded he has known more happy moments than any prince on earth. His natural spirits gave him rapture with his cookmaid, and cheerfulness when he was fluxing with a garret.[4]

Mary was tough as well as loving. She compared him to Richard Steele, (remembered affectionately in *A Journey from This World to the Next*, as 'a very merry spirit' (*J*. 38)). Although Fielding had more learning and genius, she saw them as alike in that they 'always wanted money in spite of all their friends, and would have wanted it if their hereditary lands had been as wide as their imagination'. Yet, she concluded, each of them was 'so formed for happiness, it is a pity they were not immortal'.

In Fielding's writing, openness to experience, deep learning, and wide sympathy are combined with inventive wit, exuberant imagination, and a daring approach to form. These qualities, matched by his sorely tried optimism about human nature – and his gift for happiness – make him a humane and moral novelist, and a great one.

Notes

PROLOGUE

1. Anthony Ashley Cooper, 3rd Earl of Shaftesbury, *Characteristics of Men, Manners, Opinions and Times* (1711), ed. John M. Robertson (2 vols. in one; Indianapolis and London: Bobbs-Merrill, 1964), i. 72. Quoted in the excellent discussion of Shaftesbury and Mandeville in relation to aesthetics in David H. Solkin, *Painting for Money: The Visual Arts and the Public Sphere in Eighteenth-Century England* (New Haven: Yale University Press, 1993).
2. Thomas Hobbes, *Leviathan* (1651), bk. 1, ch. 13, ed. C. B. Macpherson (Harmondsworth: Penguin, 1951), 186.
3. Ibid., bk. i, ch. 16, 217.
4. 'Essay on Eating', *Universal Spectator*, 21 Aug. 1736. Quoted in Martin C. Battestin, *Henry Fielding: A Life* (London: Routledge, 1989), 149–50.

CHAPTER 1. YOUTH, PLAYS, AND POLITICS

1. Ronald Paulson, *Hogarth* (3 vols., Cambridge: Lutterworth Press, 1992), i. *The Modern Moral Subject, 1697–1732*, 172.
2. *The Complete Letters of Lady Mary Wortley Montagu*, ed. R. Halsband (3 vols; Oxford: Oxford University Press, 1966), iii. 66.

CHAPTER 2. TOWARDS FICTION: THE *CHAMPION* AND *SHAMELA*

1. Arthur Murphy, 'An Essay on the Life and Works of Henry Fielding', prefixed to vol i of the first edition of Fielding's *Works* (London, 1762), 28.
2. Alexander Pope, *The Dunciad* (1728), in Herbert Davis (ed.), *Pope: Poetical Works* (Oxford: Oxford University Press, 1966), 472.
3. *Champion*, 4 Oct. 1740. Quoted in Battestin *Henry Fielding*, 284.

CHAPTER 3. FORM AND FALSITY: *JOSEPH ANDREWS*

1. Judith Frank, 'The Comic Novel and the Poor: Fielding's Preface to *Joseph Andrews*', in *Eighteenth-Century Studies*, 27/2 (1993–4), *passim*.
2. 'Preface' to Sarah Fielding, *The Adventures of David Simple: Containing an Account of his Travels through the Cities of London and Westminster in Search of a Real Friend* (1744), ed. Malcom Kelsall (Oxford: Oxford University Press, 1969), 5.
3. William Hazlitt, 'Henry Fielding', in *Lectures on the English Comic Writers*, in P. P. Howe (ed.), *William Hazlitt: Complete Works* (21 vols.; London: Dent, 1930–4), vi. 106.
4. Michael McKeon, *The Origins of the English Novel, 1600–1740* (Baltimore: John Hopkins, 1987), 401.

CHAPTER 4. VICE AND VISION: *JONATHAN WILD* AND *A JOURNEY FROM THIS WORLD TO THE NEXT*

1. Dr George Cheyne to Samuel Richardson, 9 Mar. 1741–2, quoted in Roland Paulson and Thomas Lockwood (eds.), *Henry Fielding: The Critical Heritage* (London: Routledge, 1969), 118.
2. Claude Rawson, *Henry Fielding and the Augustan Ideal under Stress* (London: Routledge, 1972); 209–11. David Nokes adopts Rawson's argument in his introduction to the Penguin edition of *Jonathan Wild* (Harmondsworth: Penguin, 1982).

CHAPTER 5. WAR, WOMEN, AND WORLDLY JUDGE-MENT: *TOM JONES*

1. Lady Louisa Stuart, 'Introductory Anecdotes', in Lord Wharncliffe (ed.), *The Letters and Works of Lady Mary Wortley Montagu* (2 vols.; London, 1861), i. 106.
2. Prose paraphrase of Ovid's *Ars amatoria*, quoted in Battestin, *Henry Fielding*, 412.
3. This argument is put forward by Angela Smallwood in her illuminating book, *Fielding and the Woman Question* (Brighton: Harvester Wheatsheaf, 1989), *passim*.
4. Samuel Johnson, *The Rambler No. 4*, 31 Mar. 1750, included in Paulson and Lockwood (eds.), *Henry Fielding*, 233.
5. Henry Fielding to Samuel Richardson, 15 Oct. 1748. Quoted in Battestin, *Henry Fielding*, 442–3.

CHAPTER 6. PRISON GATES: THE *ENQUIRY* AND *AMELIA*

1. A mock autobiography in the journal *Old England*, quoted in Pat Rogers, *Henry Fielding: A Biography* (London: Paul Elek, 1979), 166.
2. Stephen Copley (ed.), *Literature and the Social Order in Eighteenth Century England* (Beckenham: Croom Helm, 1984), 11.
3. Quoted in Rogers, *Henry Fielding*, 191.
4. George Eliot, *Middlemarch* (1871-2), ed. W. J. Harvey (Harmondsworth: Penguin, 1965), 194.
5. John S. Coolidge, 'Fielding and "Conservation of Character"', *Modern Philology*, 57 (1960), included in Ronald Paulson (ed.) *Fielding: A Collection of Critical Essays* (New York: Prentice Hall, 1962), 169–73.

CHAPTER 7. FROM COVENT GARDEN TO LISBON

1. Samuel Johnson in Hester Lynch Piozzi, *Anecdotes of the Late Samuel Johnson* (London, 1786). Included in Paulson and Lockwood (eds.), *Henry Fielding*, 445.
2. Colley Cibber, *An Apology for the Life of Mr Colley Cibber* (London, 1740). Included in Paulson and Lockwood (eds.), *Henry Fielding*, 115.
3. Rawson, *Henry Fielding*, esp. 18–19.
4. *Letters*, ed. Halsband, 87–8.

Select Bibliography

WORKS BY HENRY FIELDING

Collected Editions

The Works of Henry Fielding Esq.; with the Life of the Author, ed. A Murphy, (4 and 8 vols.; London, 1762).

Henry Fielding: Complete Works, ed. W. E. Henley (16 vols.; London: Heinemann, 1903). This is still the most useful source for some minor works, especially the drama.

The Wesleyan Edition of the Works of Henry Fielding, ed. W. B. Coley *et al.* (Oxford: Clarendon Press, 1967). This authoritative edition, still in progress, has detailed general and textual introductions, and comprehensive annotation. The following works have already appeared (listed in chronological order of publication in Fielding's lifetime).

Joseph Andrews (1742), ed. Martin C. Battestin (1967).

Miscellanies: Volume One (1743), ed. Henry Knight Miller (1972).

Miscellanies: Volume Two (1743); ed. Bernard A. Goldgar (1993). Includes *A Journey from This World to the Next* (1743).

The True Patriot and Related Writings (1745–6), ed. W. B. Coley (1987).

The Jacobite's Journal and Related Writings (1747–8), ed. W. B. Coley (1974).

Tom Jones (1748), 2 vols., ed. Martin C. Battestin and Fredson Bowers (1974).

An Enquiry into the Causes of the Late Increase of Robbers and Related Writings (1751), ed. M. R. Zirker (1988). Includes *A Charge to the Grand Jury* (1749), *Examples of the Interposition of Providence* (1752), pamphlets on Bosavern Penlez (1749) and Elizabeth Canning (1753), and *A Proposal for Making an Effectual Provision for the Poor* (1753).

Amelia (1751), ed. Martin C. Battestin (1983).

Covent-Garden Journal (1752) and *A Plan of the Universal Register Office* (1751), ed. B. A. Zolger (1988).

The following editions of individual works are also recommended.

Plays

The Author's Farce (1730), ed. Charles B. Woods (London: Edward Arnold, 1967).

The Tragedy of Tragedies (1731) and *Tom Thumb* (1730), ed. L. J. Morrissey (London: Oliver and Boyd, 1973).

The Grub-Street Opera (1731), ed. Edgar V. Roberts (London: Edward Arnold, 1969) and L. J. Morrissey (London: Oliver and Boyd, 1973).

The Historical Register for the Year 1736 and *Eurydice Hiss'd* (1737), ed. William W. Appleton (London: Edward Arnold, 1968).

Fiction

Joseph Andrews and Shamela (1742, 1741) ed. Douglas Brooks, (Oxford: Oxford University Press (World's Classics), 1971); ed. Homer Goldberg (New York: Norton Critical Editions, 1987).

Jonathan Wild (1743, 1754), introduced by A. R. Humphreys with commentary by Douglas Brooks (London: Dent (Everyman), 1973); ed. David Nokes (Harmondsworth: Penguin, 1982).

A Journey from This World to the Next (1743), introduced by Claude Rawson (London: Dent (Everyman), 1973).

Tom Jones (1748), ed. R. P. C. Mutter (Harmondsworth: Penguin, 1966); ed. Sheridan Baker (New York: Norton, 1973); ed. Claude Rawson (London: Everyman, 1991).

Amelia (1751), ed. David Blewett (Harmondsworth: Penguin, 1987).

Miscellaneous works

The Female Husband and Other Writings (1746), ed. Claude E. Jones (Liverpool: Liverpool University Press, 1960). Includes *The Masquerade* (1728).

Covent-Garden Journal (1752), 2 vols., ed. G. E. Jensen (Oxford: Oxford University Press, 1915). Detailed introduction on 'The Paper War' is still useful.

The Journal of a Voyage to Lisbon (1755), included in the Everyman *Jonathan Wild* (see above, 1973).

The Criticism of Henry Fielding, ed. Ioan Williams (London: Routledge, 1970), A useful collection of essays and statements.

BIBLIOGRAPHIES

Battestin, Martin C., 'Fielding', in A. E. Dyson (ed.), *The English Novel: Select Bibliographical Guides* (Oxford: Oxford University Press, 1974).

Hahn, H. George, *Henry Fielding: An Annotated Bibliography* (Metuchen, NJ: Scarecrow Press, 1979).

Morrissey, L. J., *Henry Fielding: A Reference Guide* (Boston, Mass.: G. K. Hall, 1980).

Henry Fielding: An Annotated Bibliography of Twentieth Century Criticism, 1900–1977 (New York: Garland, 1980).

BIOGRAPHIES

Battestin, Martin C., *Henry Fielding: A Life* (London: Routledge, 1989). Undisputed authority with regard to fact but questionable on interpretation of Fielding's intellectual and religious beliefs and personal life.

Cross, Wilbur L., *The History of Henry Fielding* (3 vols.; (New Haven: Yale University Press, 1918).

Dudden, F. Holmes, *Henry Fielding: His Life, Works, and Times* (2 vols.; Oxford: Clarendon Press, 1952).

Rogers, Pat, *Henry Fielding: A Biography* (London: Paul Elek, 1979). Highly recommended: lively, scholarly and sympathetic.

Thomas, Donald, *Henry Fielding* (London: Weidenfeld and Nicolson, 1990). A substantial and measured account.

CRITICAL AND CONTEXTUAL STUDIES

This section lists useful books and a small selection of recent articles indicating current critical perspectives. In the mid-1980s debate focused on Christian–Humanist readings (Battestin), and on stresses in the 'Augustan ideal' and in the aristocratic tenor of Fielding's writing (Rawson). Recently, particular attention has also been paid to the political/legal dimensions (McCrea, Bell, Richetti, Stephanson); feminist analysis (Smallwood, Scheuerman); cultural context (Colvin); the problems and politics of the genre (McKeon), and conceptual and stylistic disjunctions in character and narrative (Castle, Frank, Wilner).

Agnew, Jean-Christophe, *Worlds Apart: The Market and the Theater in Anglo-American Thought, 1550–1750* (Cambridge: Cambridge University Press, 1986).

Alter, Robert, *Rogue's Progress: Studies in the Picaresque Novel* (Cambridge, Mass.: Harvard University Press, 1964).

—— *Fielding and the Nature of the Novel* (Cambridge, Mass.: Harvard University Press, 1968).

Battestin, Martin C., *The Providence of Wit: Aspects of Form in Augustan Literature and the Arts* (Oxford: Clarendon Press, 1974).

Bell, Ian, *Literature and Crime in Augustan England* (London: Routledge, 1987). Useful cultural history of representations of crime: literary, pictorial, and legal.

Blanchard, F. T., *Fielding the Novelist* (New Haven: Yale University Press, 1926). Helpful account of Fielding's critical reputation.

Bloom, Harold (ed.), *Henry Fielding: Modern Critical Views* (New York: Chelsea House, 1987).

Booth, Wayne C, *The Rhetoric of Fiction* (Chicago: University of Chicago Press, 1961).

—— *The Rhetoric of Irony* (Chicago: Chicago University Press, 1974).

Butt, John, *Fielding* (Writers and their Work, First Series, no. 57; London: Longmans, 1954). Vivid, concise, and scholarly.

Castle, Terry, *Masquerade and Civilization: The Carnivalesque in Eighteenth-Century English Culture and Fiction* (London: Methuen, 1986). A superb, intricate reading of *Amelia*.

Copley, Stephen (ed.), *Literature and the Social Order in Eighteenth-Century England* (Beckenham: Croom Helm, 1984).

Costa, Astrid Masetti Lobo, 'Up and Down Stairways, Escher, Bakhtin and *Joseph Andrews*', *Studies in English Literature*, 31/3 (1991), 553–68.

Frank, Judith, 'Literature, Desire and the Novel: From *Shamela* to *Joseph Andrews*', *Yale Journal of Criticism*, 612, (1993), 157–74.

—— 'The Comic Novel and the Poor: Fielding's Preface to *Joseph Andrews*', *Eighteenth-Century Studies*, 27/2 (1993–4), 217–34.

George, Dorothy M., *London Life in the Eighteenth Century* (London: Kegan

Paul, 1925). Still unrivalled for detailed context.

Harrison, Bernard, *Henry Fielding's Tom Jones: The Novelist as Moral Philosopher* (Brighton: University of Sussex Press, 1975).

Hatfield, Glenn W., *Henry Fielding and the Language of Irony* (Chicago: University of Chicago Press, 1968).

Hulme, Robert D., *Henry Fielding and the London Theatre* (Oxford: Oxford University Press, 1988).

Hunter, J. Paul, *Occasional Form: Henry Fielding and the Chains of Circumstance* (Baltimore: Johns Hopkins, 1975).

—— *Before Novels: The Cultural Context of Eighteenth Century English Fiction* (New York: Norton, 1990).

Lewis, Peter, *Fielding's Burlesque Drama: Its Place in the Tradition* (Edinburgh: Edinburgh University Press, 1987).

McCrea, Brian, *Henry Fielding and the Politics of Mid-Eighteenth Century England* (Athens, Ga.: University of Georgia Press, 1981).

—— 'The Social Élite in *Joseph Andrews*', in Donald C. Mell (ed.), *Man, God and Nature in the Enlightenment* (East Lansing, Mich.: Colleagues, 1988).

McKeon, Michael, *The Origins of the English Novel, 1600–1740* (Baltimore: Johns Hopkins, 1987). Theoretically sophisticated, politically oriented re-siting in relation to New Historicism, Marxism, Foucault, and Bakhtin.

McKillop, A. D., *The Early Masters of English Fiction* (Lawrence, Kans.: University of Kansas Press, 1956).

Nussbaum, Felicity, and Brown, Laura (eds.), *The New Eighteenth Century: Theory, Politics, English Literature* (London: Methuen, 1988). See Jill Campbell on gender and impersonation in the drama, and John Richetti on servants and proletarians.

Paulson, Ronald, *Satire and the Novel in Eighteenth-Century England* (New Haven: Yale University Press, 1967).

—— (ed.), *Fielding, A Collection of Critical Essays* (New York: Prentice Hall, 1962). Useful collection of important early and mid-twentieth century essays, including Empson, Digeon, Sherburn, Coolidge, Middleton, Murry.

—— and Lockwood, Thomas (eds.), *Henry Fielding: The Critical Heritage* (London: Routledge, 1969). Excellent collection of early criticism, including informal comment and letters.

Price, Martin, *To the Palace of Wisdom: Studies in Order and Energy from Dryden to Blake* (New York: Doubleday, 1966).

Rawson, Claude, *Henry Fielding: A Critical Anthology* (Harmondsworth: Penguin, 1973). Selected criticism, eighteenth century to 1970s.

—— *Henry Fielding and the Augustan Ideal under Stress* (London: Routledge, 1972). Provocative and useful close readings, especially of *Jonathan Wild*, in relation to contemporary thought.

—— *Order from Confusion Sprung: Studies in Eighteenth-Century Literature from Swift to Cowper* (London: Allen and Unwin, 1985). Stimulating on the drama, *Amelia*, and Empson's '*Tom Jones*'.

Richetti, John, 'The Old Order and the New Novel of the Mid-Eighteenth Century: Novelists and Authority in Fielding and Smollett', *Eighteenth-Century Fiction*, 2 (1990), 203–18.

—— 'Class Struggle without Class: Novelists and Magistrates', *The Eighteenth Century: Theory and Interpretation*, 32, (1991) 231–80.

—— 'The Public Sphere and the Eighteenth-Century Novel', *Eighteenth-Century Life*, 16 (1992), 114–29.

Scheuerman, Mona, 'Henry Fielding's Images of Women', *The Age of Johnson*, 3 (1990), 231–80.

Shortland, Michael, 'Setting Murderous Machiavel to School: Hypocrisy in Politics and the Novel', *Journal of European Studies*, 18/2 (1988), 93–119.

Smallwood, Angela, *Fielding and the Woman Question* (Brighton: Harvester Wheatsheaf, 1989). Slightly over-programmatic but valuable rereading, grounded in contemporary debate.

Solkin, David H., *Painting for Money: The Visual Arts and the Public Sphere in Eighteenth Century England* (New Haven: Yale University Press, 1993). Interesting on Fielding and Hogarth, 'character', and high and low culture.

Spacks, Patricia M., *Desire and Truth: Functions of Plot in Eighteenth-Century Novels* (Chicago: University of Chicago Press, 1990).

Stephanson, Raymond, 'Fielding's "Courts": The Legal Paradigm in *Tom Jones*' *English Studies in Canada*, 14/2 (1988), 152–69.

Van Ghent, Dorothy, *The English Novel: Form and Function* (New York: Rinehart, 1953). Good on form and language in *Tom Jones*.

Watt, Ian, *The Rise of the Novel* (London: Chatto & Windus, 1957).

Welsh, Alexander, *Strong Representations: Narrative and Circumstantial Evidence in England* (Baltimore: Johns Hopkins, 1992). Interesting long section on *Tom Jones*.

Williams, Ioan, *Novel and Romance, 1700–1800: A Documentary Record* (London: Routledge, 1970). Contemporary comments on Fielding and others.

Wilner, Alene Fish, 'Henry Fielding and the Knowledge of Character', *Modern Language Studies*, 18/1 (1988), 181–94.

Index